Dating
and the
50-Year-Old Man

**True Stories of a Middle-Aged Man's Quest
for Romance and Love in Today's World**

Stephen Hemmert

Dating and the 50-Year-Old Man
True Stories of a Middle-Aged Man's Quest
for Romance and Love in Today's World
By Stephen Hemmert

ISBN-13: 978-1-4774103-2-5
ISBN-10:1-4774103-2-5

Cover design and photographs by Sarah Hemmert
Chapter page illustration by Irina QQQ/Shutterstock
Layout and additional artwork by Lighthouse24

Table of Contents

Foreword

There are few mirrors in the world that provide us with as clear a reflection of ourselves, our needs, desires, fears and self perpetuated illusions ... as the intimate exchanges we attract, and occasionally push to prolong in the relationship realm. In *Dating and the 50-Year-Old Man,* Stephen Hemmert takes us on a deeply compelling and captivatingly honest quest for the same sweet, simple and satisfying love that eludes so many. His refreshingly frank and entertaining account of his pursuit for partnership after having been unexpectedly thrust into single hood, is as socially and culturally revealing as it is poignant. Men will surely be elated to see that they are not alone in their titillating and sometimes tiresome tribulations in romance. Women have an extraordinary opportunity to walk in a good man's shoes and perhaps through his observations, which include the side-effect of sexual empowerment on courtship, reconsider their own roles in relationships in lieu of asking if chivalry is dead. Overflowing with humility and heart, this book openly shares chapters of a life with the kind of intimacy and truth, which remind us that the hope, curiosity and desire for love truly unites us all.

Charly Emery
Author of *Thank Goodness You Dumped His Ass*

Preface

The pain felt after we lose the love of our life to another, is one of the most difficult and heartbreaking experiences a human being can feel. The method and length of mourning for this lost love is always an individual event. Some may linger for a short period of time and some for month's, years, even a lifetime.

This book is about my unexpected journey into the world of dating after the breakup of a relationship I thought, like many do, would last a lifetime. The women, and the things that happened here are absolutely true. You might find some of the stories and events humorous, and even hard to fathom, and others painfully sad.

The search for romance and love has never been an easy road and once you become middle aged it becomes even more difficult because your needs, expectations and requirements become clearer and even a bit jaded. This makes the possibilities of finding the right person even more daunting. And what about finding your "soul mate"? Some might say, forget about it. But I believe she's out there. And, she's waiting for me. We just have to find each other in the maze.

The world has changed immensely since my foray into dating in the 1970's. We had no Internet, cell phones, smart phones, I-pads. Heck, we didn't even have pagers.

Our line of communication was a landline phone, or we wrote a letter or, dropped by to see each other face to face. We usually met a potential mate at the store, work, clubs, and school or through friends. With the advent of Internet dating sites, meeting someone should be so much easier right? Well, according to Datingsitesreview.com, it is estimated that there are over 1,500 dating sites in the United States alone and 54 million single people. 5.5 million have tried Internet dating. 33% formed a relationship with someone, 33% have not and 33% quit Internet dating altogether. Even with this 2.1 billion dollar industry assisting us to connect with each other, failure to find a relationship is still in question. Why is that?

One potential reason, at least from the Internet perspective is that 81% of online daters lie about themselves. Many do so to fit with what they believe the other person maybe looking for. So, in reality, they are not being true to themselves and that will lead to a false and misleading relationship. So, if the Internet is not reliable, where do you find a partner? Sadly, there are no absolute methods or answers to this age-old question.

At the conclusion of this book, I wish I could tell you where and how to find love but I can't. I can only pray that I somehow stumble upon that magic formula so that I can not only find what I seek, but that someday, I might be able to help others find their "other" half. I wonder sometimes, if I am destined to exhaust all the methods that don't work, to be able to discover the ones that do? While there is wisdom and knowledge in personal life experience, versus theory or someone else's advice, I know I must choose a different path to finding what I want than the road I have chosen so far. Ah, life's little lessons.

I believe in an all encompassing, ethereal love and I know we have many soul mates to fulfill that wish. I am passionate about finding her but I also know the more you chase your dreams or things, the farther they seem to move away. As if your neediness and energy are just too great. So, I am no longer chasing anything. Instead, I simply relax into the space of already possessing it. I have come to learn that visualization and assuming that you already have what you want, is critical to getting it. If you don't believe that you already have what you want, you create the "lack of" which drives your desires even further away. The theory of getting what you want is, you ask for it, work at it and be open to receive it when it appears. Now that last part is critical, as we may not recognize the person when they arrive because we are still stuck on finding them. We can't see the forest for the trees or, they may not look or resemble the person we setout to find. That is a conundrum. We have to be open to the possibility the person may not physically appear or initially act like what we envisioned. However, we have to look deeper into ourselves and in them to find the true connection. Many, including myself may not take the time or do the work to find the greater gift of the person if the packaging, or other elements of the person are not in alignment with what we believe we want or desire.

It's like judging a book by its cover. It must appeal to us somehow for us to pick it out of thousands of other books. But what if we chose it not because it was pretty, or sexy, or visually appealing but in some way strangely unique, maybe even a little odd or out of place. Then, like you are doing right now, we read the preface and we see what the author is about and what they have to say. Now we find this person even more intriguing than the odd cover we were somehow attracted to in the beginning. Then we feel compelled to purchase this book even though the story may not be something we would normally be attracted to or desireth of. We take the book home, we read it chapter after chapter and we suddenly find ourselves wrapped up in this person's words, passion and stories. We finish the book and draw a long, deep breath and say to ourselves. "How had I not found this book before? It's nothing like I have ever seen, read or experienced." This sort of thing opens our eyes, our minds and our spirit to the gift of "allowing" or as I simply call it, being "open" to the possibilities. We found something that stirred our soul, captivated our mind and now helps us see the world in a completely different way and this is good. I would like to think what occurred here is intuition. Not some accident or mistake, but a gut feeling to pickup that ugly little book and without consternation, buy it and discover its allure and message. To find it's greatest gift was inside.

As for me, I told God, the universe, and myself that I was open to wherever life would lead me. It was this being "open" to things, along with many other elements, that allowed me to attract, date and in some cases, fall in love with the women in this book.

Now that I have been there, done that, I am focusing on attracting the one and only into my life. So, when I go to sleep at night, I envision and actually breathe in the feelings and emotions that I want to find in my mate.

I imagine how she feels in my arms. The lovely smell of her hair and her soft luxurious skin. I envision looking into her eyes and seeing my own soul illuminated within. I feel in every part of my being the electricity that occurs as our bodies meet, flesh to flesh and our hearts beat in perfect rhythm together. As my hand lies gently on the curve of her back, we kiss we melt into each other's soul, like two scoops of ice cream melting in a bowl. I imagine us having long deep, spiritual conversations and yet, laughing our asses off at the silliest of things. Of us being of one spirit, one energy and understanding each other before we even speak. Rolling with each other even when one does not want to roll. Ebbing and flowing together in almost perfect harmony and light. Supporting each other in times of trouble or fear. I try and assimilate all these things and more into my being so I can really know what it means to be in love and to find my other half.

Fantasy you say? An Illusion? Poetic nonsense? Absolutely not. For what in life starts without a dream, inspiration, or passion? We must, as human beings and spirits, seek expression and ever growing desire to discover new things in life and more importantly, in ourselves.

In the mean time, I hope you enjoy this book and my strange yet joyful journey into the world of middle aged dating. Here's to love, wherever it is found.

Sincerely,
Stephen Hemmert

Acknowledgements

I want to thank all of my amazing friends and family who stood by me during the moments I needed them most. In many cases, I had to lean on them for support, motivation and, most of all, love.

It's funny how life leads you in directions you never dreamed of or thought you wanted to go. But, I have learned so much about the subconscious self that it has trained me to really respect and understand that part of me that may not speak loudly or even make itself known. This is where self-awareness really begins.

Many of my friends and family have heard my crazy stories and thought that I was probably headed for the loony farm. Looking back, I see that they had reason to be concerned. But, with their love and understanding, I survived the trip. I don't know if they realize it, but they also went on this journey with me, albeit vicariously. Again, I love you all.

A big thank you to Hay House Incorporated for granting me permission to use quotes from the wonderful Abraham series of books by Jerry and Esther Hicks. All Jerry and Esther Hicks quotes are the property of Hay House Inc. Carlsbad, Ca.

Prologue

This book should be easy to write, but it isn't, even though the incidents and events are true. Yes, there may be some embellishments to make a point or drive home a particular message, but everything on these pages happened to me. The women are real, not fabricated characters from my imagination.

Okay, so what's the point of this book? First off, for me, it is an important sense of expression and, in a way, closure. We, as humans, have to find ways of channeling and expressing ourselves. If not, we are a stewing, angst-ridden, powder keg of pent up emotions. So, here it is. My words pouring onto the page, like water splashing from a boiling pot.

Some might wonder why I would write about the most negative and odd behaviors of male and female interactions. But then, are we not more intrigued by the odd things in life than the ordinary ones? Just look at all the cop and detective shows on TV and the incessant flow of reality (un-real) shows. No one would watch them if they featured normal people. But, if you showcase some weird, crazy little human beings, you have a hit.

After reading this book, some of you may think that I'm an excessively horny, womanizing philanderer with no soul. My history, prior to this period in my life, was one of monogamy, commitment and dedication. I'm a sensitive, romantic man who simply wants to love and be loved, just the same as everyone else. But, finding love in this day and age is not an easy task. In fact, love can be painfully hard and seemingly impossible to find.

Not to be negative or paint a bad picture of romance and love, but ask any single person how difficult it is to find someone. You would hear many horror stories similar to ones that I will share here. I also want to clarify something. I am not the tall, dark, handsome model on the cover of GQ. I am not a millionaire, in fact, not even close. I drive a nice car and my home is just an average house. I work in the food service industry as a commissioned salesman and I have credit card debt and financial challenges like everyone else. Overall, I am an average Joe in just about every way except that I am very confident about my talents and abilities and passionate about the things I love in life. I have a wacky sense of humor and my kids would be the first to tell you that the character "Austin Powers" was written about me. In fact, I love to do impressions of various characters and some of my favorites are from the Austin Powers movies. Humor and being able to laugh is critical in life. I feel that having a good sense of humor is appreciated by most women and maybe that's part of my allure. I just love to have a good time and make people laugh.

Also, everywoman I approached or flirted with I did not wind up dating. Some didn't think I was their type and that's Okay. Rejection is a part of everything in life and especially in the world of romance. But I also did not date every woman that approached me. That said, the women mentioned in this book are the ones that stood out and in many cases blew my mind.

A Little Background

Before launching into women and relationships, or the lack thereof, I feel like I should provide a little background that inspired me to write this book.

I was married to a woman named Jessica for sixteen years and it took another seven until our divorce was final. I had married my best friend. We had so much in common that it was hard not to be attracted to each other. On top of that, she was quite attractive. One common bond we shared was the same birthday; we were exactly ten years apart. I was a starving musician when we met and she was a college student, on the verge of dropping out of school. Neither of us had two nickels to rub together and, in retrospect, maybe that was another commonality and the impetus for us to join together and flourish in some way.

So, in October, 1984 we got married. I got a part-time job in the mailroom of an insurance company while I continued to work on my music career. Jessica, after dropping out of college, took a job at a medical supply company. A few years later, tired of starving and trying to keep a band together, I resigned my dream of being a rock star and concentrated on getting a job that actually paid a decent wage.

In 1987, I took a job with a startup company in Hollywood, thanks in a large part to my buddy, Larry, who worked with me at the insurance company. His father and another creative soul were starting a telemarketing company. Though I despised telemarketing, I would be working in the computer and human resource side of things. It paid off and the company grew from five people to over 1800 by the time I left.

Jessica and I finally had the money to live a good life and we started a family. Our first child, Brianne, was born just six months before my father died. She was the first grandchild in my family and I was blessed my father got to see and hold her before he passed away from cancer. Four years later, Michael was born. Had he held onto the womb just two more days, he would have been a Scorpio, just like his sister, mother and I. Can you imagine four Scorpios in one house? Thank God he ended up being a Libra.

Jessica ended up working in real estate and she went back to college to get her degree. When she completed that, she went on to get her Master's. The telemarketing company sold to a group of investors from the East Coast and I left to pursue other things. I learned to make wine and plant and grow grapes with my friend, Enrique. I played golf, spent more time with the kids and worked on my idea to start a wine and cigar bar. I have to say, that the day I left the telemarketing company was one of the most glorious times in my life. I finally knew what freedom was. Of course, it didn't hurt that I had negotiated a nine-month, full pay and insurance from the company. I learned the joy and freedom in having money and the ability to do the things you love to do.

We started a little place on Ventura Blvd. in Studio City called Sonoma Blue. The goal was to create a wine and cigar venue where you could try and pair different

California wines with appetizers and sample great cigars from around the world. Well, the wheels fell off right after getting the building ready to open, due to a wonderful California law that read, "no establishment serving alcohol could be located within 600 feet of a church, school, playground or hospital." We certainly didn't have any of those nearby. So, where was the issue? It turns out that an old bank that was located only 300 feet away had been converted into a church called "In His Presence." In an instant, the original dream of the wine bar was pronounced dead.

Stubborn as I was, I would not be defeated and I changed the focus to coffee and desserts with bistro-styled food. Though not even close to my dream or intent, the idea took off and became, for a while, a success. It was this grasping for straws idea that created the best of times and absolute worst of times for me. But, I learned that the contrast of desires can help one focus on what one truly wants and does not want. And that helped me get through it all.

My mother, Dottie, moved in with us in order to watch the kids while I worked insane seven-day-a-week hours and Jessica pursued her Master's. Thank God for my mother. Mom had lost sense of the world when Dad passed away and it was her grandchildren that made life worthwhile for her. She was a great babysitter and influence on our kids. I'd like to think they had a great influence on her, as well.

Sonoma Blue had morphed into a performance venue, mostly due to the need to capture more business. We had entertainment almost every night of the week. One night would be stand-up comedy, another acoustic music, poetry and my favorite, Open Mic nights, which were held on Friday and Saturday. We were packed with singers, musicians, poets, puppeteers, comedians and odd balls. We were the talk of the town.

Sonoma Blue was located next to a famous dance studio called "Morrow Landis," which had been there for nearly 50 years. From that venue, we received our biggest clientele and numerous famous persons paid us a visit. Tony Danza, Paula Abdul, Kelsey Grammar, Jon Voigt, Tim Matheson, Beck, K.D. Lang and many, many others passed through our building. Sonoma Blue was a work of passion, but it never made much money. Yet, it was home to a lot of wonderful people who drank coffee, hung out and performed there. Many of the customers are still great friends of ours today and our lives have been enriched by all of them.

But, while wonderful things were happening at Sonoma Blue, other things became intolerable. There was Al, our business neighbor, who tortured us every way he could in order to drive us out of business so that he could buy the building. A Starbucks opened across the street, severely cutting into our business. And, worst of all, my marriage was beginning to decay. The marriage issue began to surface when I hired an employee to help out at the coffee house. Jessica approved of her hiring and liked her a great deal. I had no idea, nor did they, that their rapport would turn into something much more. They fell in love.

There are things in life that you can control and there are things that seem to be destined and written in the stars, no matter what your actions or wishes are. This was one of them. In working and striving so hard for things, Jessica and I had lost each other. It was a tumultuous time and having to see the two of them together at the restaurant was very hard to handle. However, I believe that regardless of your feelings and pain at any time, God truly has a better – or at least a different – plan for your life which you may not be capable of seeing in that swirling mess of ego and emotions inside of you. The struggle with moving on comes from the difficulty of letting go of the ego and anger, while finding a place of acceptance to see the possibility of a blessing.

Jessica and I separated and the kids took it very hard. They were in a conundrum. They liked her partner, but were sad that Dad and Mom were no longer together. Jessica moved to an apartment behind the coffee house and I remained in the house in Santa Clarita. Thankfully, I got to see the kids all the time at the coffee house and had them on the weekends. But, that too would end.

After the opening of the Starbucks across the street, the harassment by Al got even worse. He called every agency he could to get us closed down. The proverbial shoe, which had been hovering just above our heads for so long, finally dropped. The dance studio building was sold to, you guessed it, Al. Not only did we lose hundreds of next-door customers, but he closed the building for over a year. By this time, I was dead broke and borrowing money from my mother to pay the mortgage. I took a job with a large food distribution company to begin a new career in food sales while still working at the coffee house. I was getting four hours sleep a night and I was losing weight, as well as my mind. In August 2000, I closed the coffee house, said a tearful goodbye and filed bankruptcy to try and save what was left of my possessions, life and dignity.

After closing Sonoma Blue, I felt a great sense of relief and yet, sadness. Yes, I loved the place and the people I met there, but there are times where we have to follow the path of least resistance. I took a position as a Sales Associate for a large food distribution company and tried to reconstruct my shattered life. Selling food was not what I wanted to do with my life, but my former food sales rep., Joy, who was married to my brother, talked me into it. It was a whole new world for me, as I had never worked as a sales person. It paid off quite well for me though and I became a President's Club member only a year after being hired.

Shortly after starting with the company, I met a woman who would change my life forever and, in a sense, is a huge reason this book was written.

Mary

I met Mary on the Internet, where she had posted a profile on Yahoo's dating site. I didn't trust the Internet to be a way of finding a relationship, but the minute I saw her picture, something in my soul told me I had to meet her. Mary was a beautiful, African-American woman whose dating preferences fit me to a T. She was looking for what I believed to be me: a white male who was artistic, driven, but also able to stop and smell the roses. She wanted to meet someone who was not hung up on sports or watching TV, someone who wanted to experience life, travel, was able to hold a conversation and was on a spiritual path.

I matched her requests in every possible way. There was only one problem: she never returned my messages. I wrote her three times to exclaim how perfect I was for her and yet, nothing. Finally, I sent one more message, saying that she at least owed me a response. I asked her how in God's name could she not see that I was perfect for her. She finally responded one day, saying that her experiences with three other dates on Yahoo were horrible duds and that she had, in fact, cancelled her listing, but at the last minute, due to a dream, decided to write me, after all. What ensued were hours on the phone with each other and nights together in long conversations about life, death and spirituality. We had even read and were reading many of the same books on those topics.

I felt I had found my true soul mate and there was nothing I wouldn't do for her. I remember the first time she came to my house for dinner, after a few dates. I took all the roses in my yard and pulled off each petal. I took the petals and placed them along the walkway so that when she arrived, she would be lead to my door by the bright red petals. Call me a hopeless romantic, but that's the way I felt about her.

Mary moved in with me six months later. Of course, I talked to my kids about her and then, had them meet her for their approval. They were reluctant, but Mary had the type of personality that she could talk to anyone. My kids ended up liking her, as she was open and communicative. I got their OK, though they were not excited about her moving in.

The real estate market in southern California started to boom in and around 2002. I had lived in the house nearly 16 years when Jessica requested we sell it. I disagreed, not wanting to uproot the kids' history and lives any further and to give them some bastion of stability and comfort. However, her need of the proceeds from the sale of the house was required, as was my need to let go and move on. This was no longer our home; it was simply a house that contained only memories and nostalgia. After all, why is the fear of something new so scary?

The house went up for sale in December 2002. It sold in one day and the buyer wanted a 45-day escrow. This presented a problem, as Mary and I had little time to look for something new and I had my nearly 80-year-old mother to think about and look after. I didn't know if she would be able to handle a change in residence after suffering a broken hip and the illnesses she already had. Mom was not well. Though her mind was as bright as ever, the resurgence of post-Polio syndrome and kidney failure was pushing her to the limit.

Mary and I looked for weeks and weeks for a house I could afford. The market had exploded and everything decent was beyond my price range. One day, we looked at a house on a hill in rural Agua Dulce. Though, it needed a lot of work, both of my kids, who went on this expedition with us, agreed that it was the one. And, so it was. I made an offer and got the house, including $10,000 in cash from the owner to clean up the property. Lee, the owner, raised and sold birds of all types and sizes and had bird cages and pens in every conceivable spot. Along with the birds and their nasty little excretions, came rats, squirrels, mice, gophers and all other critters that ate all of the food the owner threw out to the stinky, feathered creatures.

I had moved my mom into a motel for over a month while we waited on the escrow on the new home to close. Mary and I had moved in with my friend, Enrique, until we finally got the keys to the house on March 23, 2003. That's when the work began. We started cleaning, painting, fixing and converting the garage into a livable space for my mother, who smoked a pack a day. We worked like a real team to not only clean up the place, but to care for my mother, who by now needed almost constant attention. Dottie who loved to talk, cherished Mary and they would chat about anything and everything. They were best buddies until her passing in November 2003, just days before my 49th birthday.

Mom's death hit all of us hard. She was a loving, authentic character with a lot of spirit who was raised in racist, rural Arkansas to distrust and avoid dealings with "colored people", as they called them back then. Mom said to me numerous times that she had never met or associated with black people and yet, both my brother Dino and I were with black women. Mom finally learned, before her death, that the color of one's skin has no real significance on who they are. It's the character of one's spirit that truly matters. I know she was in heaven, watching with a smile on her face as her services were carried out by a black minister with many black people in attendance.

Work on the house and property continued after my mother's passing. Side by side, Mary and I planted a vineyard, put in a pool, built a deck and lay sod in the yard. Mary was an amazing artist and she created a warm, spiritual resonance of our life together on the walls of the house. Celtic ruins were painted along the top of the living room walls, along with a large, magnificent sun on one wall. A fresco of wine bottles and grapevines graced the kitchen where I built a bar. We were teammates, friends and lovers. We were spiritual seekers, educating and helping each other along the path. But then, like many things in life, that changed.

After work on the house was completed and things calmed down, we lived a good life together and yet, problems began to surface. Mary liked a secluded, quiet life and hated intrusions or disruptions. She had issues with my kids coming to visit, which was odd since she had such a good relationship with them before. She had more issues with the fact that Jessica and I had yet to divorce, as well as the influence that Jessica had in our lives because of the children. Mary was changing. I sensed dissatisfaction in her, not only because of Jessica and the kids, but also me and life, in general. The sense I got from her was that she felt her job here was done.

And, so it was. We parted in November 2006. Although I knew it was for the best, I was devastated. I had never experienced a soul like hers. I was so enamored with her that I loved to just lie in bed and watch her talk. I loved the way her mouth moved when she spoke and the deep soulfulness of her eyes. The beauty of her caramel skin and the way she spoke with such passion and conviction... I was completely and forever in love with her.

This is where the story really begins. In losing Mary, I lost myself. But, soon, I began to wonder if maybe I had discovered my real self. Read on, you tell me.

Saying Goodbye

I remember that day like it is happening at this very moment. It's almost as if I can still feel the knot that was in my stomach when Mary told me about Maurice. We had been separated for a few months before we decided to give it another chance once I got back from taking my daughter to the Bahamas for the Semester at Sea program. After all, things were different. Mary had moved into her own house and was at peace with her quiet, tranquil, solitary life. We could actually have fun with each other without the ties of living together. However, things like that rarely work. I think I knew that, deep down. How can you go backwards when you have already come so far down the road together? I still loved her and enjoyed her company, so I figured it was worth a try.

Shortly after my return from the Bahamas, she decided to go on a five-day cruise to Mexico and asked me to go with her. I had already missed ten days of work and there was no way could I get someone to cover for me again. As she got ready for the cruise, I said, kiddingly, "Don't you go falling for somebody on the ship!"

She laughed and pointed out that she was going with her spiritual books to read and relax. She called me a couple of times from the ship to say she wished I was there with her and that she was having a good time.

At that time, I was just learning to read Tarot cards and, whether you consider them to be accurate or nonsense, I did a reading on Mary and her cruise. Maybe it was because I sensed something I couldn't explain. I asked the question to the cards, "Please give me insight on Mary and our relationship." As I selected and placed three cards, one representing the current situation, a second placed to show the past and a third to represent the potential future, I got an answer that reverberated in my already suspicious consciousness.

The first card, representing the present, blew my mind. It was the "Knight of Wands." This Knight represents a male over 40 who is confident, sexy and seductive, attractive to women, full of energy, starts things, but fails to finish them, passionate, but impatient and understands others. Not only did that card say to me that Mary may have met someone, it was the future card that said it all. "The Lover's Card" represents attraction, the beginning of a romance, good times, close friendships and adventures. I was breathless for a second. Cruise and adventures? Could she have fallen in love or lust with a man who represents the Knight of Wands? I brushed off the notion. I was just learning to read Tarot and, for all I know, it's just folly.

When she returned, we met at my house and talked about her trip. She told me she had met a lot of cool people on the cruise and, in particular, a piano player who she said reminded her of me.

"His name is Maurice and he's charismatic and bald like you. He plays piano and sings; he's funny and tells jokes. I couldn't believe how much he and you are alike," she said.

Something felt odd about her statement, but I couldn't place what had bothered me about it. Then, I remembered the Tarot card reading.

"Did you sleep with him?" I asked her.

"No, but the people at my table and I had drinks with him after his show."

Somehow, as I had known her for five years, along with my odd feeling about the card reading, I didn't buy her answer and yet, I had no cause to doubt her.

To celebrate being back together, we decided to have a party at my house where we would invite our families and a few friends. Since my brother is a drummer and I play guitar and piano, I figured we could have a jam session. A friend of Mary's dad came over with his bass guitar and, after a five-course meal I prepared, we played for hours and everyone had a great time. But, when the night ended, I felt that a certain darkness had set in. Mary, instead of lending a hand with the cleanup, decided to criticize how I loaded the dishwasher, among other things. When I asked her to assist me in cleaning up, she said that it was my idea for the party and she did nothing to help with the aftermath. Something was not right with her and I would soon find out what.

We went to bed exhausted and we fell asleep in a heartbeat. The next morning, I had to deal with a problem with the kitchen sink that had decided to clog up and overflow. I noticed Mary had her camera and she started taking pictures of the watery disaster and then, she moved inside and outside the house, taking random photos.

"What are you doing?" I asked her.

"I'm taking pictures of all of Stephen's disasters."

She then showed me the pictures of the deck where I had spilled some cement while laying my beautiful rock floor for the master bedroom, the rusting washer and dryer that was in the laundry room and the disheveled music room with drums, amps, guitars and office equipment. I looked at her.

"Why are you pointing out all the negative things?"

That's when she uttered, "I have something I need to tell you."

Those words hit me like a bolt of lightning and my stomach tied itself in knots. Have you ever had someone say something so simple and yet, so devastating? Well, I did and it turns out I was right. We sat at the kitchen island and she began to tell the "true" story of the cruise vacation.

"I have to be honest about what really happened. I didn't tell you everything. One night, I didn't feel like going to dinner, but it was my last night on the ship, so I decided to go. I sat at a table with a married guy and a couple of women whom I had dined with before. They were good people and we had a fun time together. After dinner, we all went to the bar where there was a piano player."

"Maurice?" I interjected.

"Yes. We all sat and listened, drank and had a great time. As he closed his show, he announced to the crowd that he was crazy about a girl in the audience and he pointed at me!"

"And?"

She thought and slowly continued.

"We all went to the bar for drinks and a bite and we hung out. When everyone else went back to their cabins, Maurice and I continued to talk."

"About what?" I mumbled.

"About him, his life and how he got into music. Also, about me and me being an artist... and if I was single."

"What did you tell him?"

"Well, I told him that you and I just got back together, but I wasn't sure if it was going to work."

I was shocked and she met my expression with sadness.

"So, you basically gave him an open door, didn't you?" I asked.

"Let me finish. We talked about spiritual things and I thought we had a lot in common. During our conversation I told him I wanted to get some dental work done and he said he knew of a great dentist and we exchanged phone numbers."

I started to laugh and she looked slightly embarrassed.

"Mary, he's on a cruise ship in Long Beach. You live in Castaic, an hour and half away and you have to get the name of a dentist from him when there are so many nearby?"

"Well, he's been calling me and we have been talking on the phone for hours."

"And?"

"He's asked me to come to see him on the ship."

"What did you say?"

She looked at me with those big, liquid brown eyes and, in one sentence, tore my heart from my chest.

"Stephen, I want to pursue it."

Emotions began to well up inside me.

"So, you want to date him?"

"Yes, I want to give it a shot."

After regaining my breath and what dignity I still possessed, I looked at her and said, "Well then, pursue it."

"I'm sorry, mi amor; it's something I want to do," she said.

Maybe I was still in shock, but shortly afterwards, I proposed what might have been the worst idea in the history of man and relationships.

"I bought us tickets and reserved a room for a couple of days in Napa. Do you still want to go? We can make it our last date."

Mary stared at me for a while and said, "Yes, that sounds fun."

At that moment, I should have saved myself from the upcoming misery I was to endure by taking my shotgun and ending it all right then and there, figuratively speaking, of course. But, I find it interesting that only love can cause such pain and agony. If I didn't love her or care for her, nothing could hurt this way. I read in many spiritual books that only through true love can you experience true pain and true joy. Well, guess which one I was feeling.

The Trip from Hell

Mary reluctantly met me at my house for the flight to Napa early in the morning on a Friday. Days before, she had protested that I should pick her up at her house, but I refused. The reasoning was that I was only thirty minutes from the airport and her house was thirty minutes in the opposite direction and, by God, if she couldn't accommodate me after I spent the money and offered the weekend vacation, she could stay at home and I would go on my own.

When she arrived, there was no warmth or excitement in her. I, too, was in a strange place, emotionally, and was thinking how big a fool I was for doing this. Tasting wines in Wine Country is one of my greatest passions and I know I should have taken this trip alone, but I didn't. When we got to the airport and were boarding, I asked her to do me a favor.

"Mary, this is our last moment together and all I ask is that we don't talk about Maurice and your relationship with him."

"OK," she responded.

I had brought my Tarot cards with me as I was learning to read them like my father's mother had. When I was sixteen, my grandmother predicted I would have a long life and live into my 80's. Well, that's yet to be proven, but I hope it's true, as long as I am in decent health and still have my wits about me.

Soon, after the plane took off, Mary began to do just what I had asked her not to. She started to talk about her trips down to see Maurice in Long Beach. I asked her to stop and remember her agreement, but the desire to torture me was too great. She explained how it took almost an hour and a half to two hours to get there and that they could only see each other outside the cruise ship. I turned a deaf ear, but my brain continued to process her words.

"We have no place to go, so we would hang out at restaurants or in my car," she said.

"In your car?"

"Yes."

"What did you do in your car?"

She had no problem letting me know.

"Made out and had sex."

Jesus, am I a gullible fart or what? My stomach started to hurt and I turned away, so she wouldn't see the pain on my face. Thankfully, it was a short flight to Oakland from Burbank. We found our rental car and were going through the gate when a large, cheerful, woman took our paperwork and stared at me. I was confused as to why she was gawking at me.

"Anybody ever tell you that you look like Bruce Willis?" she asked.

"Yes, I've heard that before."

"Damn. You sure do look like him."

I thanked her and we were on our way. Of course, I had lost some zest for spending time with Mary by now, but the wine and the rolling hills of Sonoma and Napa were calling.

We arrived at our motel in Napa called the "Wine Valley Lodge", which was built in the early 50's or so and it was reported that Elvis had stayed there while filming his movie, *Wild in the Country*. It was a plain and yet, very warm and comfortable place.

Mary, who I always thought was sexy and attractive, decided to seduce me. It wasn't tough to do. I was a willing participant; after all, this was the last time we would be together. I kicked myself later for succumbing to her that day because that's how women use their feminine allure to garner power and control. Once a woman gives herself to you, she feels you owe her or that she owns you.

We showered, changed clothes and headed out to taste wine and, hopefully, have a decent time. We started in St. Helena at Stony Hill for a private tour and tasting, as I knew one of the owners. We sat on the patio, enjoying wonderful Chardonnay, Riesling and Gewürztraminer.

We later hit Caymus, Silveroak, Stags Leap and a couple of others before heading back to the motel and to dinner. Mary behaved herself and I was starting to forget about the rough start to the trip. Later that night, we had dinner at some totally forgettable steakhouse. The conversation during dinner was difficult and trite. I guess I didn't really have much to say, nor did I want her to say too much, as I was afraid it would have wandered into the topic of her and Maurice. We headed back to the motel and went straight to bed. Little did I know that the weekend was going to get much worse.

Saturday came and we heard on the news that a portion of the main freeway in Oakland, the 180, had collapsed after a tanker truck had caught fire and the cement and rebar holding the bridged section melted and fell. That was our freeway back to the airport, so now we had to allow a lot more time to get back and, in the process, lose precious wine time.

We ate a continental breakfast at the motel and headed to explore some wineries I had never been to. We started at Rombauer in St. Helena, which is my favorite winery for Zinfandel. As we approached the winery, Mary's cell phone rang. My intuition instantly told me it was Maurice. As she answered the phone, her eyes immediately shot my direction.

"Oh, hello, Maurice."

I slumped in my chair as my heart landed in my ass. I could hear him speak to her and she didn't try to hide the conversation at all.

"Where are you?" he asked.

She looked my direction.

"Napa."

"What are you doing there?"

"I'm with Stephen," she replied.

"Does he know about me?"

"Yes."

"Is he OK with that?" Maurice nervously questioned.

"Yes, I think so."

At that point, I looked at her, flipped her off and got out of the car. I slammed the rental car door so hard that the car shook for a moment. I quickly walked into the winery as she continued to stay in the car to talk to her new lover.

After about twenty minutes, she came into the tasting room and put her hand on my shoulder, which I gently pushed away.

"Come on, we're leaving," I said.

"I wanted to taste wine!"

"Well then, you should have been inside with me instead of talking to dickhead Maurice in the car."

I told her to get in the car and that I was taking her back to the airport and dropping her off with only the clothes she had on. As we drove off, she tried a half-assed apology and said that Maurice only gets a few hours off the boat and she had to take the call or miss talking to him for a few days. Needless to say, there was no pity from me.

"Fuck Maurice," I shouted. "You would rather insult and hurt me than miss talking to someone you just met! What kind of person are you?"

I was so hurt and angry that I could have run us into a Goddamned tree, but I didn't. I was in my favorite place in the world and I was living a nightmare.

My mother taught my brothers and me to never go to bed angry or hateful, but to place a smile on your face for, if you should do so, your dreams will be pleasant and you will wake up happy. I loved that saying and I tried to do as she instructed, but as I went to bed that night, I just couldn't. My heart was in pain and my mind was festering with anger and insult.

Sunday, our last day in the wine country and our last day together, finally came. I was still reeling from the prior incident, but I wanted to make this last day as good as possible, so I thought as positively as I could. That didn't last too long, however.

As I walked into the bathroom to take a shower, Mary asked if she could borrow my computer to check her artwork that she had on eBay. I gave her the computer and I went about my bathroom business. Upon reentering the bedroom, Mary greeted me by asking if I wanted to see Maurice.

"What?"

"Here he is," she said proudly, as she turned the computer around to show me his web site and him playing a song on piano.

Not just any song, but "Great Balls of Fire", a song I also performed at every company and family event. I was devastated at her rudeness and lack of sensitivity. I shut the computer and told her to get her things. I was taking her back to the airport to dump her ass off and come back. Then I remembered... the damned freeway was closed. Shit.

I went off the charts emotionally and I told her that she was cruel and I would not treat an enemy the way she just treated me. She looked at me like a little kid getting scolded by her parents. She showed no remorse, only a deer-in-the-headlights look, as if she had no idea why I was so upset. I took a moment to get my composure back before speaking to her again.

"Hurry up. Get ready. I need a fucking glass of wine."

We headed out to the Sonoma Courtyard. There were many great places to eat and, within a short distance, one of my favorite wineries, Buena Vista. Being a wine member there, they treated the two of us like royalty. We got to try many of their wonderful and flavorful wines. The setting was beautiful and it is the oldest premium winery in California. The cellar and wine tasting room were like a history lesson waiting to be discovered.

After Buena Vista, we enjoyed Ferrari-Carano, St. Francis, Kenwood, and then retreated back to Sonoma for a late lunch before heading to the airport. As we sat eating, I began to tear up. Yes, the wine does make me a more sensitive soul, but as I watched the sunset behind the rolling hills of Sonoma, I realized our love and partnership had also slipped away.

The trip to the airport was painfully slow with the freeway closure, but we got there. We sat in the airport with little to say. It was an eerie feeling because we always had something to talk about. Now, there was nothing.

After arriving to the Burbank airport, the ride to my house to pick up her car was also uncomfortable. When we got to the house, I took her bag out of the trunk and placed it into her car. She gave me a hug and apologized about the weekend and her being a bitch. I hugged her back, knowing that soon, she would be with another man.

"Goodbye, mi amor," she said.

She gave me one last kiss, got into her car and drove away with my memories and my heart.

I often wonder why people have to be so cold and hurtful to each other at the end of a romance. After much soul searching and meditation, now I know that we have to create a reason or excuse for our actions. What I mean is that if you poison the well, you know you can never go back and drink from it. That would not be reasonable. If you damage a relationship bad enough, you know there is never any going back, never a way to repair what that has been done. That gives you freedom to move on, as that is the only choice that remains. I think of the old Viking philosophy, which states something similar to, "Burn all the ships upon our landing. There is no turning back."

My Personal Awakening

S o, the split with Mary began an awakening for me on many fronts. First, it taught me, once again, that nothing in life is permanent. Second, it taught me that Paramahansa Yogananda was right in his teaching that human love is fickle and fades over time, unlike the undying love of God. And third, I learned that I still had it. Had what? I still seemed to be attractive to women. In fact, something amazing happened. Not since my days in rock and roll had I received the attention of so many women. I can only attribute this to the fact that I was confident, and bound and determined to show Mary and, more importantly, myself that I could find someone just as pretty, smart and more loving than her. I was also open. What I mean is I allowed the universe to lead me wherever that took me. That attitude led me to the experiences and women I encountered.

It's funny, when you are determined and committed with all your being, things can and do happen. I've always heard that women can sense confidence a mile away and, in fact, are quite attracted to it. So, I put my swagger into high gear and set my sights on dating as many women as I could.

I had no real intention of finding a true replacement for Mary, at least, not yet. I simply placed my emotionally scarred heart into a tamperproof safe and stepped back into the world of dating. In the next chapters, you will meet many women that I had the pleasure and good fortune of meeting, spending time with and, in some cases, sharing intimate moments. Some are the jewels of the universe and salt of the earth. And some are... just completely messed up. Lost souls who believe that happiness is only found in the presence of someone else, when in reality, happiness begins and ends inside of us. If one is miserable with oneself, how in God's name is one going to find happiness elsewhere? It's impossible.

Although I was happy with my life and who I am, I still attracted these women and so, I am responsible for much of what happened. In fact, I learned more about myself than I ever expected. A friend told me, "Only through our relationships can we truly know who we are."

This book chronicles my dating life from May of 2007 until February 2011, almost four years. If someone was to win my heart, they had to blow me away like Mary did. When I met her, there was absolutely no doubt in my mind she was "it." You don't have to think about whether you love someone or not because you will feel it in your very soul and with Mary, I did.

I know the mind is a very powerful influence that can talk us into and out of just about anything. However, it is the spirit and heart that always remains true to our self and which should be followed. Unfortunately, many times, we do not heed our internal feelings. Some of my choices in women were made not by my instinct, but by other realms of Stephen. Was that a mistake or a great opportunity for a lesson?

There is a saying that I believe to be true: when someone leaves you and breaks your heart, nothing heals it faster than finding someone new. This new person and adventure helps take the pain and sting out of our memory. The trouble is, I set the bar so high in what I then wanted to experience that almost no one could match my requirements and desires.

Wine and Women

Women are like wine to me. I use my expertise in winemaking here to note that I classified many of these women by virtue of the grape I think they most represented. You may see me mention this here and there. Like a grapevine, it can be born and raised in very different soils, climates and conditions. It can have a long, distinguished lineage or one that's not so respected or admired. The vine can produce grapes of extraordinary flavor, beauty and complexity, or the exact opposite. Also, each varietal has characteristics that separate it from others and this I most noticed in the women I dated. No two were alike, although some had the same growing conditions, terroir and similar nuances.

Lastly, I want to note that the women in this book, except for one or two, came onto me sexually and not the other way around. This is not to say I didn't partake or enjoy it, but like I say throughout the book, I was blown away at the aggressive nature and sexual freedom of these women. In fact, I was in shock at some of their ideas and suggestions. No, I am not a prude, but as I was experiencing my newfound freedom, so were these women and they were not afraid to make sex and intimacy a reality, even if only temporarily.

Jezebel

Although I promised myself to get back out there and start dating, in truth, I needed time to lick my wounds and let them heal. But, fate steps in when sometimes you release all resistance to things. I was taking the food order from one of my customers, Martha, from "Dinners to go." Once the order was done, she held up her right hand.

"Oh, I almost forgot," she said. "I have two tickets for you to "Taste of the Town" this coming weekend. Would you like them?"

"Sure, I have my son this weekend, I'll take him."

She then reached into her file folder and pulled out a couple of tickets and handed them to me.

"You never know, you may meet somebody."

I thanked her again and left with a feeling that she just might be right.

My son, Michael, and I boarded the tram from the parking lot when I noticed a lovely, black woman in a beautiful, yellow summer dress sitting in front of us. Michael saw me looking at her and rolled his eyes and smiled.

Getting off the tram, we picked up our tickets to give the vendors for food and beverage. The beautiful, park-like setting was hopping with all kinds of interesting people. A band playing 70's and 80's hits provided the soundtrack to the event and it was what you could call a perfect day.

Michael and I made the rounds tasting and enjoying all the wonderful food. As we rested at a table, I felt the need to visit the little boy's room. A row of porta-potties lined an area of the park and I headed that direction while Michael held down the fort.

As I walked toward the plethora of chemical toilet buildings, I saw to my left a beautiful, well-endowed, yet petite woman. I couldn't take my eyes off her. She was fair-skinned with black hair and engaging features. Of course, my eyes saw her two largest and most pro-nounced features as she approached me. To be honest, I slowed down a bit to allow her to catch up to me. As she did, being the gentleman I am, I offered her the first open porta-potty.

"Here you go," I proudly stated.

"Wow, what a gentleman, thank you," she said, in a slight Latin accent.

"My pleasure."

As she entered the porta-potty, I quickly grabbed the next open one and proceeded to talk to myself.

I wonder what her name is. I didn't even look to see if she was married. Shit, why didn't I look at her finger? Maybe it was because you were looking at her breasts? Yes, of course. That's why. Stop lollygagging she might be already done. Hurry up and get out there.

As I flew out of the porta-potty, I nailed a passerby, who was not too happy.

"Watch it!" he yelled.

"I'm sorry," I shot back.

I looked around, but didn't see her. As I washed my hands at the wash station, someone tapped me on the shoulder. I turned around and there she was.

"Hello," she said, softly.

"Hey," I answered, dumbly.

"I want to thank you again for being so nice and letting me have the porta-potty. There are not many gentlemen left these days."

"Is that so?"

She placed her hand on my arm and said, "I'm Jezebel."

"Oh, hey, I'm Stephen."

I looked into those dark, intriguing eyes and lost where I was for a moment. However, she got me back on track.

"I hate porta-potties," she said. "I have this deep fear of them."

"Really, why?"

"I just hate being crammed into a smelly, hot, little nasty plastic building."

I shook my head in agreement.

"You know what is funny? I didn't even have to go to the bathroom."

"Then, why did you?"

"My friends set me up with this deadbeat, horrible blind date and I was trying to get away from him, so I could call my friends and tell them how pissed I was. Shit, there he is! Come on, walk with me. Pretend that we are talking business or something."

We sauntered towards a man who was dressed in jeans, an Izod shirt and white boat shoes. He looked to be much older than my newfound friend. She was right; her friends screwed her on this one.

"His name is Frank. Quick, give me one of your business cards."

I dug into my wallet and handed it to her just as he met up with us.

"Frank, this is Stephen. He works for Super Foods and I thought my company might be able to use his services."

"Hey there, Stephen, I'm Frank," he announced, as he strongly shook my hand.

"Glad to meet you," I responded with as much bravado.

Frank smiled uneasily at me and turned to Jezebel.

"Well, are you ready to enjoy the rest of the day?"

She looked at me as if to say, 'save me please', but she held it together and turned to him and said, "Sure."

As they walked away, Jezebel turned back to look at me and I began to laugh as she gave the 'gag me' hand sign and then, the 'call me' gesture.

I was glowing as I walked back to Michael and the table.

"Why were you gone so long?" Michael inquired.

I could only mumble, "I just met an angel."

"You met an angel in the toilet?"

"Yep, and I hope she calls me."

"What if she doesn't? Did you get her number?"

I looked at my teenage son and feeling silly and responded.

"No, damn it."

Then, with a strange, newfound confidence I made a brash statement.

"She'll call. You just watch."

Michael rolled his eyes and looked off towards another food vendor.

"Come on, Dad, I'm still hungry. Let's try the sausage place over there."

As we walked away, I desperately looked for her, but lost her in the sea of people. But, somehow, I knew I would see her again.

Back home, I decided to check my phone messages at work and, lo and behold, there was a message from Jezebel.

"Where did you go? I was looking all over for you after I ditched the date from hell. Here's my cell number. Give me a call; I'd love to chat with you."

I wrote down the number and smiled ear to ear. Although the pain of my split with Mary was present, I still felt honored that someone thought I was attractive and worth pursuing.

I called her back and we set a date for Friday at one of my accounts, TGC, a private golf course with some of the best dining in the city. I let Chef John know that I had met Jezebel at the "Taste of the Town" event and he cordially invited me to bring her to the club for dinner on him.

Jezebel looked stunning in her colorful summer dress when I arrived at her door.

"Hola, Chico," she said in that Latin accent of hers.

"You look amazing."

"Thanks, baby."

Her voice was so interesting. It was appealing and yet, a little difficult to get because of the quick and rapid manner in which she spoke.

"Where are you from originally?" I asked her.

"Well, Porta-potty Steve – that's what I'm going to call you from now on – I'm from Cuba baby, can't you tell?"

She smiled and then, did her impression of the actress, Charo.

"Coochie, Coochie!"

She laughed at her own silliness, grabbed her sun hat and away we sped in my BMW z4 convertible. She remarked about what a beautiful and sexy car it was. I have to say, regardless of what we may want to believe, the car a man drives does matter to many woman. Illusion or not, I've heard women friends of mine explain that the car the man drives not only speaks of the attitude and character of the man, but also about the way they may feel about him and the potential relationship. Now, hopefully the person that owns and drives the nice car has enough substance to transcend the initial attraction of the car, but that is up to the one riding in the passenger's seat.

We arrived at the club and I proudly escorted her into the dining room. Not long after reaching our table, I pulled out a bottle of my own wine. A 2005 Zinfandel I had made from grapes in the Santa Maria area of the Central Coast.

The waiter brought us two glasses and opened the wine, pouring some for me first to assure it was worthy of my guest. He then poured her a glass and then, topped mine off. Jezebel tasted the wine.

"Wow, this is nice," she said. "What is the winery?"

I turned the bottle to expose the label, which, of course, proudly displayed "Stephen Hemmert Vineyards."

"This is yours?"

"Yes, it is."

"Wow, so you make wine too?"

She nodded her head in approval and smiled. At that moment, Chef John came to greet us.

"Glad, you made it," he said.

I stood to shake his hand.

"Chef John, this is Jezebel."

He bent towards her and took her hand, and in the calm voice he is known for, greeted her, "Jezebel, pleasure meeting you. You are very beautiful"

Jezebel smiles and blushed at his statement.

"So, have you had a chance to look at the menu?" Chef asked.

"No, I think we need a few moments." I stated.

"OK, well when you're ready let the waiters know."

Chef John walked away, only to turn and look at me with a big smile on his face. I assumed she earned his seal of approval.

We ordered and talked all the way through dinner nonstop. Jezebel had no problem expressing her views on life, so the evening was everything you could ask for, except for one annoying thing: she kept answering and texting on her cell phone. She said it was her son, who is ten, and I had no cause to doubt her.

After dinner and wine, I was beat. Friday was tough for me, as I had to be in meetings in Oxnard, California at seven a.m., which was an hour and a half from my home. Pulling into her driveway, she turned and gave me a kiss and asked if I would come in for a glass of wine.

"I'm so tired, I don't know if I should," I weakly replied.

"Ah, come on, just one glass of wine," she persisted.

As she opened the door, her son and another child appeared to make sure it was she and not someone trying to break in. She was surprised to find him in her face as she pushed the door open.

"Oh, you scared me!" she shouted.

"Sorry," her son replied.

I entered the house feeling a little uneasy. This was a first date and I was not sure I was ready to meet her children.

"Eli, this is Stephen."

"Oh, hey," he said.

"Nice to meet you, Eli," I said, shaking his hand.

"Eli, introduce your friend."

He quietly and reluctantly told me his friend's name, which I instantly forgot.

"Okay, go back to doing whatever it was you were doing," Jezebel said.

He waved goodbye and they disappeared into his bedroom.

Jezebel's house was a work of art. Not so much in its grandeur or size, but in the way she had it decorated. It was full of beautiful and exotic African masks and trinkets, not to mention the extraordinary taste she had in furniture.

"Wow, your place is beautiful."

"Thanks."

"Where did you get these amazing masks?" I asked, as I perused the variety of authentic hand-carved pieces.

"A friend of mine in San Diego has an import business and he gets me good deals on them."

"I bet some are very expensive," I stated as I looked at a mask that was huge and adorned with hair and feathers.

"Some are up around two to three thousand dollars." she shouted from the kitchen.

"Impressive."

Jezebel appeared carrying two glasses of white wine and sat them on the coffee table.

"Come, sit." she asked as she plopped down on the sofa.

I did as instructed and took a sip of wine. She scooted a little closer to me.

"Do you like the wine?" she asked.

"Yes, it's nice. A chardonnay from Sonoma, I suspect?"

"Yes, it is Buena Vista Winery."

"No kidding? That is one of my favorite wineries."

"Mine, too. You know, I have always dreamed of living in Sonoma and owning a house with a small winery, a red barn and a beautiful vineyard."

"No way, seriously?" I asked.

Jezebel looked puzzled at my questioning her.

"That's my exact dream, down to the barn." I informed her.

I was astounded that someone I just met could have the same dream as I. It should also be said that Jezebel and I shared the same exact birthday, November 10th. Two hot-blooded, sensual Scorpios, dreaming the same dream. Wow!

We talked as we sipped our wine and time disappeared. The next thing I knew, Jezebel was kissing and caressing me. I, of course, kissed her back. Everything was fine until she climbed on top of me and straddled her legs over mine, kissing me with even more fervor. She began to dry hump me and I became very nervous about her son hearing this heavy breathing and thumping of the couch against the wall.

"I don't think we ought to be doing this with your son next door," I whispered.

"He's fine, he will stay in his room," she said between kisses.

We continued and suddenly, she took my hand and placed it on her large firm breasts. I had not been on the dating scene for a long time – after being married for sixteen years and with Mary for another five – and I was shocked and a little dismayed that I didn't have to work a little harder to get this far.

"Jezebel, we need to cool it," I informed her.

"Why?"

"Because I'm not comfortable with your son being in the next room and I am really tired. I need to go."

She gave me a kiss and got off of me. I stood up and straighten up a bit, except down below I was already quite straight enough.

She took the empty glasses back into the kitchen and came back out to say goodbye. She kissed me again and walked me towards the door. As I reached for the doorknob, I turned to say goodbye and she grabbed me and rammed her tongue down my throat. I put my arms around her and kissed her back. She then took my hand and placed it on her ass.

Nice ass, I thought to myself

When she began to grind against the lump in my pants, I had to pull away.

"Baby, I have to go," I said.

"Are you sure you can't stay here with me?"

"No, some other time, maybe."

I kissed her and again, grabbed the doorknob. As I opened the door, she gave me one last kiss and I walked out towards my car.

"I had a good time. Drive safe," she shouted.

She stayed at the door until I was gone. As my heart raced, little Elvis – the name I gave my penis – returned to normal size. I asked myself what had just happened. I wondered if she was really that attracted to me or was she just horny? Was she really that free with herself, especially with her son and company next door? Did we really have the same dream? Had I entered the Twilight Zone?

Weeks later, I saw her again. The result was similar, but this time we were alone at my house and so what developed... um... developed. She is a very sexual and open-minded creature and that was very much a turn-on for me and yet, I felt she was too aggressive. Sex and intimacy with Mary was... well, not all that intimate or consistent, so I was enjoying this newfound sexual expression and experience, yet still concerned everything was going so fast.

It made me ask myself if I had actually found someone for me this quickly. My attraction to her was not just from the sexual perspective, but also from the fact that we also thought a lot alike. Jezebel was energy, sensuality and intelligence, all wrapped into a voluptuous, five-foot frame. She and I shared the same humor and excitement for life. But, the truth was my heart was closed off to her. She was wonderful, but I simply wasn't ready to get into a relationship yet. And then, fate intervened.

Jezebel took a job with a company out of state and was moving. The day she told me, many things ran through my mind. I realized that I really liked this woman and she seemed to really like me. There could have actually been potential if this head on my shoulders could let go of the past and somehow find the key to unlock my heart.

There was another thought that I had, as well, which was, whew, that was a close one. I almost got involved with someone again. Saved by the bell.

Once she moved, we stayed in touch for a while. I often wonder where the relationship might have gone had she stayed here. But, that's the thing with fate. It leaves a lot of what ifs.

When I compare her to a particular grape variety, I sometimes think she would be a champagne or, as we have to call it in California and all of the United States, a sparkling wine. She was like a Chardonnay-driven bubbly. This is because she was light-skinned and full of energy, wild like the bubbles escaping upward from the glass that holds the nectar. She aroused my senses and was bursting with energy and life.

After her, came a litany of women and crazy encounters. It's almost as if I asked God and the universe to experience every psychologically twisted woman with a titanic-sized load of baggage to come into my life. I must have asked because I do believe we attract things to us. And to do that, the vibrations and need for life experiences have to match.

Dominga

Not long after Jezebel moved out of state, I met a woman at one of my accounts, The Cork, a local wine bar where, in truth, I met many of my potential dates.

I was there for a Wednesday night wine tasting event when I saw her sitting at the bar. A friend of mine, Wagner, was there and I sat next to him, with her to my left. She was on her cell phone and had an interesting accent. Both Wagner, who is Austrian, and I struggled to make out the accent. Once she was off the phone, I felt compelled to ask.

"You have a really interesting accent, where are you from?"

"Panama," she confidently and somewhat arrogantly responded.

"Oh, well, my buddy and I were trying to guess."

She turned her head back towards her glass of wine with a sort of "I'll ignore this guy" attitude.

"I'm Stephen, by the way."

"I'm Dominga."

"That's a very beautiful name. You know, I'm here a lot and I've never seen you before."

"Well, I usually come after work on Wednesday before I pick up my kids from my ex," she explained.

"Where do you work?"

"Down the street at SCV Bank."

She had soft looking, brown skin and greenish-brown eyes. She reminded me of the actress, Vanessa L. Williams.

"What are you drinking?" I asked.

"Sauvignon Blanc."

"Do you like Zinfandel?"

"No, I only like whites."

"Oh, so then you will like me." I said with a wink.

She cracked a slight, little smile and turned away. Over the next thirty minutes or so, we tried to create some kind of connection, but I could feel she had more walls around her than San Quentin prison. I gave her my business card and told her to let me know when she was back at the wine bar. She stared at my card and quickly said, "I have to go and pick up my kids."

"How many do you have?"

"Two, a boy and a girl." she said, as she picked up her purse to leave.

"Nice meeting you."

"Likewise," she replied as she turned and headed for the door.

I watched her walk away. She had a large, full rear end like Jennifer Lopez and she walked with a swing and a sway. I thought to myself, wow, she's hot, but she's a handful. She'll never call me.

A few weeks went by. I was at The Cork with my District Sales Manager finishing up a meeting with the owner, when she suddenly appeared. She walked right up to me.

"May I join you?" she asked.

My boss looked at me and got the drift.

"Hey, I need to go. You guys have fun," he said.

He packed his computer and headed out the door. She sat and smiled at me. I was captivated. There was a child hiding inside this gorgeous, strong-willed woman. That was intriguing, to say the least. The waiter came over and asked what we wanted. I ordered my favorite Zinfandel and she, of course, her Sauvignon Blanc.

"So, how are you?" I asked.

"Great, it was a very busy day at work."

"Same here."

There was a moment of silence and I asked something maybe I shouldn't have.

"So, are you divorced? Never married?"

She shot a look at me that would kill some men.

"What do you mean, never married? Do you think I am the type woman who has children out of wedlock?"

"No, I don't know you at all and that's why I am asking. I'm not making any judgments; I just wondered what your status was."

Luckily, the wine arrived and calmed the moment down. She took a sip and looked at me.

"What's your status, Stephen?"

"I am divorced; I was married for sixteen years and like you, have a boy and a girl."

She took another sip and those sultry and sensual eyes locked into mine.

"I'm divorced," she said.

"How long?"

"Five years."

One thing about me is I have to ask questions. I don't like living in the abyss, nor do I believe in deep, dark secrets that come out later to derail a potential relationship. Hopefully, the other person is actually honest in her answers.

"What made the wheels fall off?"

She looked at me.

"What do you mean, wheels fall off?"

"Oh, I mean, why did you get divorced? What happened?"

She shot me that glance again.

"I don't want to talk about it!"

I recoiled at her directness and the emotion behind it.

"Sorry, I just thought it might be something to talk about since we both have gone through it."

"No, it's nothing I want to talk about."

So, we moved on to other things. She explained how eventually she wanted to move back to Panama, once her kids were older, where she could live a better life. I hardly thought living in Panama could be better than living in the US, and especially Santa Clarita, but I sensed she felt a little lost here. Maybe that was part of her underlying anger and frustration with things.

She finished her wine and appetizer and, like the first time I met her, paid her bill, grabbed her purse and announced, "I have to go pick up my kids."

I walked her to her car and she turned towards me and gave me a hug. I was taken aback, as her hug reeked of needing comfort and intimacy and yet, her facial expression spoke the opposite. Almost as if to say, my heart is reaching out, but my mind is closed, so don't get close to me.

She got into her car and drove away, leaving me with a million questions. I did not pursue Dominga at this point. She was too much mystery and attitude for me to take on. Although, I must admit, the mystery part was quite alluring. Like the old saying goes, curiosity killed the cat. Well, I was curious, but not desperate.

About two more weeks went by and I was returning from a food show in Santa Barbara when I got a call from an unknown number.

"This is Stephen Hemmert."

"Stephen, this is Dominga."

"Oh, hey, what's going on?"

"I am headed down to The Cork and wondered if you wanted to meet me there?"

"I'm about twenty to thirty minutes away."

"No problem, I'm just getting off work, so I will see you there."

I broke the situation down as I drove. I had shown little interest in this woman and now, she is calling me. I wondered if this was the way it really worked with women these days. Show a little interest, but act like you couldn't care less? It began to make sense, especially with her. She's strong and opinionated and this is not the kind of woman you pressure into anything. She wants to call the shots.

I arrived at the wine bar and there she was, at the same table we sat at before. She already had her wine and, low and behold, she had ordered me my favorite glass of Zin.

Wow, she remembered what I drink.

I was impressed. She smiled as I arrived at the table and I placed a kiss on the side of her head.

"I hope I got you the right wine," she said.

I sipped it and it was the Rombauer Zinfandel that I indeed was addicted to.

"You did, thank you."

There was silence as we stared at each other.

"So, you look beautiful as usual," I told her.

"Thank you."

She blushed at the compliment and her eyes lit up. Now, see, here was the real her coming out of this tight, woven shell she has made for herself. I felt her soul actually start to open up; I felt her start to feel comfortable and free around me. This was exciting to witness.

"So, Dominga, what sorts of things do you like to do?"

"Well, I love to read, salsa dance and do various crafts. And you?"

"I also love to read, write, play music, grow my own grapes and make wine."

"What kind of grapes do you grow? Any whites?"

"No, I grow Zinfandel," I said as I showed her the glass filled with the magic elixir she had ordered me.

She seemed a little let down at that answer.

"I do make a sweet white wine, if you would like to try it."

"Really? What type of grape?"

"Muscat, are you familiar with it?"

"No, not really?"

"Well, I will get you a bottle to try."

I winked at her and she smiled. She opened up enough to talk very briefly about her divorce, a topic she had rigidly refused to discuss before.

It was the usual story. She, like many women, was hurt and damaged by the infidelity of her husband. She, in fact, stated that she hated him for what he did. Not just to her, but to her children. I felt her pain.

"How old are your kids?"

"My daughter, Elena, is thirteen and my son, Eduardo, is eight. And yours?"

"Michael, my son, is fifteen and Brianne is nineteen."

"Speaking of kids, I need to get going; I have to pick them up from their father."

She went for her wallet.

"I will get this," I said.

"No, I invited you and I will pay for it!" she said, glaring at me.

Surprised at the seriousness and energy of her response, I acquiesced. She paid and I walked her, once again to her car.

As we arrived at her car, I had to say what was boiling inside me.

"You know, you are an intriguing woman. But, I'm having a hard time figuring you out."

"Then, don't worry yourself about it," she spurted and turned to get in her car.

I softly put my hand on her arm.

"I don't mean this in a bad way. You are interesting, like a puzzle. You are warm, then cold, soft, then hard, happy and then sad. Why do you seem to like my companionship?"

She looked at me for a moment.

"I like you, Stephen because you listen to me and seem like you care, but if who I am bothers you, then we will drop it right here."

I looked at her guarded eyes and responded the best I could.

"No, who you are does not bother me. In fact, it fascinates me. I simply wondered why you liked me and my company."

Her face gave way to a softer, more innocent expression than she had moments before.

"Would you like to go next Thursday to the Loose Goose wine tasting?" I asked.

"I would need to do something with my kids, so right now, I'm not sure. Will you call me on Sunday?"

"Sure, but I don't have your number."

She gave me a business card for her bank and wrote her cell number on it. She hugged me once more and got into her car and drove away.

Sunday came and I was working in my vineyard all day. I phoned her around seven at night to see if she was able to go or not, as I had to purchase tickets in advance. When I called her, she was abrupt and to the point.

"It's seven o'clock and I am trying to get my kids to bed. Why did you call so late?"

I was dumbfounded as seven o'clock is not a late hour, even for school-age kids.

"I'm sorry," I replied.

There was a long pause.

"I still don't know if I can go, but I will call you Monday before eight," she shot back.

"OK, then I will wait to hear from you."

Then, she hung up the phone without another word.

What the hell, I said to myself.

Monday arrived and I never heard from her. Tuesday came and went. On Wednesday, twenty-four hours before the event, I still had yet to get a call from her. So, that evening at the wine bar, I thought she might show up since this is the time and day we usually met. When she didn't, I called her cell and she answered. Her voice was stressed and terse.

"Hello?"

"Hey, Dominga, Stephen here. I have not heard from you, so I assume you couldn't find a sitter and can't go?"

"Is that what you assume?"

"Well, you were going to call me Monday and I never heard from you, so I was unsure whether to go ahead and buy the tickets."

There was a short pause.

"If you assume I'm not going, then guess what, I'm not going!"

"Whoa, I didn't want to pressure you, but I had to find out if you could go because the deadline for getting reservations was today."

"I don't need a man like you in my life Stephen. Goodbye and never call me again!" she screamed before hanging up the phone.

The wine steward and buddy of mine, Victor, was standing next to me when this took place and heard both sides.

"What the hell was that?" Victor asked.

"For the life of me, I don't know."

Victor shook his head.

"Better let that one go," he said. "She sounds like trouble."

I was more confused about what had just taken place than I had been at any time in my adult dating life. Yes, I knew she was a complex person, but never had I experienced such a Jekyll and Hyde moment. I was always a gentleman with her. I never pushed any agenda or showed any negative actions towards her. I couldn't help but wonder if she was bipolar or in need of psychological help. On the other hand, she made it clear she hated me or at least despised me and, to this day, I do not know why.

She later became associated with a good friend of mine to whom she stated that I was a horrible person and she can't believe she wasted time on me. She never told him why she thought this or where the anger at me came from. Maybe I was getting too close and she was afraid. Maybe the wall she sometimes let down just far enough to expose her true self was too revealing and she put it back up for protection.

My friend's theory was that maybe she was falling for me and that was something she could not handle. She had to find a way out and the way she chose was to paint me as a horrible, uncaring person to whom she must avoid at all costs. She ultimately ended the friendship with him, as well, for what I assume was a somewhat similar reason.

A year or so later, I heard she mysteriously failed to report to work for three weeks and no one knew where she was. I understand later, she returned to her job, and returned back into the dating scene.

It's funny, I see her at a few wine events around town and I always say hello to her. After all, life is too short to go around hating or despising someone. She, however, won't give me the time of day. No hello, nod or smile. It's as if I hurt or maimed her in some way that still eats at her. I wish to God I knew what was going on in her head and what made her hate me so much.

She reminded me most of a Petite Sirah, made from a grape that is thick-skinned, dark in color with an ability to be either very sophisticated, full-bodied and flavorful or tannic, brooding and rough-hewn. This woman had the ability to be both types of wine produced from this one varietal.

Adrianna

I have many friends in the restaurant business, but most are men. One of my favorite customers is The Ranch Cafe, owned and run by two attractive, Ethiopian sisters, Ceela and Waana. Having known me for a long time and how happy I had been when I was with Mary, they were determined to help me forget about her and move on. Ceela's way of facilitating this was to introduce me to a woman who she said was breathtakingly gorgeous and spiritual. Ceela called me one night and asked if I would be interested in meeting Adrianna at The Cork. I said sure. After all, what did I have to lose? So, Ceela set up this clandestine meeting for a Tuesday evening.

I had not seen a picture of her, but I was told she was French and her name was Adrianna. As I walked into room, I didn't see her at first. Then, to my left, and sitting at a table in the corner, was one of the most strikingly beautiful women I have ever seen in my life. She was half black/half white and petite. I approached her.

"Adrianna?"

"Yes," she replied in slight French accent.

"I'm Stephen."

"Oh, please have a seat."

I took a seat across from her and began to give her the once over. Her long, black hair lay gently on her shoulders and her bangs were cut to expose her beautiful, green eyes and perfectly shaped face. Sometimes, I wish I were blind to such things as beauty. It throws the whole system out of whack when you also need to consider all the other elements needed for a cohesive relationship. We, guys, however, for better or for worse, are especially susceptible to this.

We ordered some wine and began to chat about ourselves. She went on to explain that she found Jesus after a string of bad luck. It seems that it is after hardships or disasters when most people find religion. Anyway, she had a bad run and here she was.

"So, what happened exactly?" I asked.

"At the age of 40, my husband had a heart attack in our house. By the time the ambulance and police arrived, he was gone."

"I'm so sorry."

"One of the cops at the scene thought I was beautiful and asked for my number."

"Are you serious? He asked for your number as your husband lay dead on the floor?"

"Yes, he was attractive, though."

"Really? You actually had the wherewithal to notice that the cop was handsome?"

"Well, things happen when they are meant to, don't they?"

"I guess, but what an odd set of circumstances." I said as I shook my head. "So, what happened next?"

She took a deep breath and explained.

"Well, I took the insurance money and opened up a dress shop on Cinema Drive. Maybe you heard of it, it was Beauty Boutique?"

I shook my head no. After all, I rarely shopped for dresses or makeup.

"I opened the shop and all was well and then, for some reason, business fell off and I had to close the store."

"I'm sorry to hear that."

"It's all for the best."

She sat up straight and there was suddenly a strength and confidence on her face that I hadn't seen before.

"Because I found Jesus," she joyfully exclaimed.

"Oh, I see... well, that's wonderful."

"Have you accepted Jesus as your Lord and Savior?" she asked, with great expectation.

I responded the best I could.

"Well, yes, I have, but I also believe that we all have the ability to communicate directly with God."

She bristled.

"No, the only way to heaven and God is through Jesus Christ."

"Okay, then what about those who are Jewish or Muslim or Buddhist? Are they not worthy of reaching heaven?"

"Absolutely not. There is one way to heaven and it is through Jesus Christ, our Lord!"

Remember the old saying; never discuss politics or religion, as no one ever convinces the other to change their minds or attitudes? At that moment, I remembered and, as I disagreed with her on the subject, I decided to let it go.

"So, do you get to go home to France very often?" I asked.

"No, not really, I haven't had the money."

The issue of money is interesting as she was dressed to the nines and had told me she drove a newer BMW SUV. Money, however, is relative to your place in life or idea about it. To some, having $10,000 dollars in the bank is a lot and to some, it is nothing at all.

She seemed alone in the world and I felt a little sorry for her.

"My friend, Enrique, owns this great country French restaurant and since Enrique and his Maître d', Claude, both speak French, would you like to go with me this Saturday? It might be fun for you," I stated.

"That would be great. Thank you!" she said, excitedly.

"OK, give me your cell phone number and I will call you to set things up."

She took out one of her old business cards for the dress shop and wrote her number down.

"I'm thinking maybe around six thirty. Is that good?" I asked.

"Oui."

I paid the bill and walked her out to her car. She did indeed own a newer white BMW SUV. It was packed with dresses and all sorts of things, as if everything from the recently closed shop wound up there. I gave her a hug good night and she reciprocated with a warm hug back. As I drove home, I could smell her sweet lingering perfume on me. It was exotic.

Saturday morning came and I called her cell phone to verify the time I was picking her up. She explained she would rather meet me somewhere and ride together to La Cuisine. That really didn't make sense to me because

I was told by my friend, Ceela, that she lived only about three miles from my house. Nonetheless, it's our first real date and I didn't want to make her nervous or freak her out. She already had a lot of crazy things happen to her and I didn't want to be another one.

I met her at her car at around six fifteen at a place a few miles from La Cuisine. She was waiting for me, dressed to kill and smelling like heaven. She got out of her SUV and asked, "Will my car be okay parked here?"

"I think so."

She looked breathtaking. Her jet-black hair framed her face perfectly and her green, piercing eyes seemed to be lit from inside. Shakespeare wrote, "The eyes are the mirror of the soul" and if that's true, then I might just like this little soul, although the religion thing was a little hard for me to swallow.

She climbed in my car and I put the top up, so as not to blow her hair into a frizzy mess. She seemed a bit nervous and withdrawn. Moments later, we were at La Cuisine where we were welcomed at the door by Enrique and his wife, Rosa. Both Enrique and Rosa were of Latin descent and spoke Spanish, so it was a little funny to be greeted in a French restaurant with an enthusiastic, "Hola, Señor Stephen!" from Rosa.

"This is Adrianna!" I announce to the two of them.

Rosa gives Adrianna a warm hug.

"I'm Rosa."

Adrianna nods her head, but says nothing. I tell them that Adrianna is from France and Enrique immediately took her hand, kissed it and began speaking to her in French. I understood a few words, as I had traveled to Paris and the Beaujolais countryside, but I could not keep up with what he was saying.

"Come this way. I understand you are dining with Enrique and Rosa and Asa tonight," Claude, the Maître d' chirped, sounding like Lumiere from the Disney movie, *Beauty and the Beast*.

We had a seat next to each other. Asa, my Swiss friend who also speaks French, was already at the table. Enrique ordered some wine and appetizers and the feast began. Enrique looked at Adrianna and then, at me with a big smile on his face and a gleam in his eyes. This was Enrique's way of saying, way to go, I approve, she's hot.

I'm not sure what happened, but when Claude brought the bread to the table, he spoke to Adrianna in French and she retorted with something very harsh and abrupt, possibly even in another language. Whatever she said had some venom and bite to it. I watched Claude roll his eyes and walk away, upset. I looked back at her to see that she remained very subdued and reserved, as if whatever happened didn't affect her.

I got up and excused myself to go to the restroom. On the way, I saw Claude and asked him what happened.

"What a snotty bitch," he spouted in his French-tinged English.

"What did she say?"

"I told her that her French did not sound like it was from Paris, but more like an influence from the countryside and the bitch told me 'I am from Paris and you don't know shit'."

"Oh, wow, I'm sorry about that," I apologized.

"She is beautiful, but I don't like her," Claude added.

In the bathroom, I thought about how chaos seemed to surround this woman and I wearily wondered what might happen next.

Enrique and Asa spoke much of the night with Adrianna, who did seem to enjoy speaking her native tongue. I couldn't get much of a word in, as her attention was on the ongoing conversation. However, I couldn't stop looking at her. I was mesmerized and I loved hearing her soft, sexy voice speaking such a romantic language.

At one point during dinner, Adrianna turned to me and said something sort of strange.

"Do you hear that?" she asked.

"What?"

"The helicopter."

I listened, but didn't hear anything.

"No, I don't, should I?"

She turned back to her plate and continued eating.

After dinner, Enrique invited all of us up to his house for cocktails and dessert. We drove to his lovely home, which was located right behind and above the restaurant. Once there, we began sampling some great old wines and even some liqueurs. Adrianna asked Rosa to go with her to the restroom. You know how women are, it takes two in the powder room. I felt they were somehow discussing me.

Adrianna appeared a few minutes later with a smile on her face and seemed more calm and relaxed. Around midnight, we called it a night and I drove Adrianna back to her car. On the way, weirdness again descended upon us.

"Do you hear it?" she asked.

"What?"

"The helicopter!"

I listened and I did hear a helicopter this time.

"Yes, I hear one now. Why do you keep bringing that up?"

"Because it's him!" she frantically stated.

"He who?"

"The cop who fell in love with me."

"The cop, who you met at your house as your husband lay dead on the floor is following you in a helicopter?"

"Yes, he has people."

As we approached her car, I had to know what the hell she was talking about.

"Why would a cop or someone in a helicopter be following us?" I asked.

"Okay, here's the deal. The cop and I started dating and we fell in love. It was not expected, but God works in mysterious ways."

"You or God works in mysterious ways?"

She ignored the question and continued.

"After finding out that cops don't make much money and he was married, I broke it off. However, he won't leave me alone. Being a cop, he can do all kinds of things."

"Such as?"

"Well, one time I was out with a guy and he followed us and pulled him over."

"For what? Speeding?"

"No, he pulled him over for no other reason than I was with him. He broke out the rear taillight and told my date that he had better take me home and if he saw me with him again, he would break something else."

"Jesus Christ!"

"No, don't use Jesus' name in vain," she spat.

"So, then what?"

"He either follows me himself or has someone else follow me at all times. He has people everywhere and I bet there was someone there tonight watching me," she said, as her voice shook in fear.

"Like whom?"

"That Claude. He's not really French, you know... he's a spy," she whispered.

"Oh, really?" I said, laughing at the thought.

"There, do you hear it? The helicopter? It's back, it's him!"

At that, I got out and ran around to her side and opened the door.

"Hey, it's been fun. Thanks for joining me tonight."

I hustled her out of the car and, as she fumbled for her keys, the helicopter seemed to indeed be getting closer. She finally found the key and opened her door. I hugged her goodbye. She gave me a kiss on the cheek and began to latch her arms around me.

"What are you doing?" I asked.

"Kissing you goodnight."

"But, the helicopter!"

"You're right, he's watching us. I better go."

"Yes, you should," I said, with the same frantic fervor.

She closed the door and drove off to wherever the hell she lives, while I prayed to God I could get home without getting pulled over by a random, phantom cop.

Adrianna and I never saw each other again, although she would call me occasionally to tell me some other harrowing thing that was happening in her life. From the constant cop chasing her, to a restaurant owner trying to rape her, to her being asked to dance nude and smuggle drugs, I never knew what she was going to say next. Finally, she stopped calling and disappeared in the abyss. I hear she has worked various jobs around town, but fails to stay employed.

Rumor also has it, she shows up at Central Park, dressed in Gucci and high fashion with her dog.

Supposedly, every guy she meets hits on her and she continues to tell people walking their dogs about cops, firemen and helicopters. Maybe what I heard about California is right: those who live here are like a bowl of cereal – whoever is not a flake, is a nut.

Needless to say, because she was French, she reminded me of a Burgundy grown Pinot Noir: soft-skinned, not overly tannic or deeply colored grape. Ultimately, a wine that, to me, possesses a nose of rose hips and flowers mixed with the terroir (the soil it was grown in) and an elegant, sophisticated long finish that symbolizes a wine of great depth. However, she was also confusing like Pinot can be. Growers in California consider it to be difficult to grow correctly to extract the proper flavors, quality and colors. She was all of that and more.

Fajia

I was having dinner at my favorite sushi place, Aomori, which was a mom and pop operation in Canyon Country. Yogi, the chef, was an affable, charming man who wore a red headband and made (still does) the best Sushi around. As I downed a glass of chardonnay with my red dragon, a somewhat interesting-looking, though not very attractive, woman began a conversation with me. She had heard me talking to Yogi about my wine making and apparently, she wanted to know more.

"So you make wine?" she asked.

"Yes, I do."

"What varietals?"

I was impressed because at least she asked what varietals and not what kind.

"I grow Zinfandel, but they are too young to harvest, so I buy grapes from the Santa Ynez area."

She nodded with approval.

"I'm Fajia and this is Michael," she said, gesturing to a young boy sitting next to her.

"Ah, Michael is my son's name, as well," I stated proudly.

"Then, we have a connection."

There was something alluring about her, although like I said before, she was not really physically attractive. But, there was the conundrum: allure is made up of many different things, not just outward beauty. But, like the French say, "Cette femme a je ne sais quoi," which means, "That woman has a certain something I cannot explain."

"Is Michael your son?" I inquired.

"No, I'd love it if he was, but he is my nephew, my sister's son."

She had a slightly raspy, smoker's voice with a British accent. She did eventually explain that she was originally from London, but was of Arab descent.

Since I was single and so was she, we decided to hang out a week later at a place in town called The Roast. Fajia and I had dinner and a few beers, which led to me learning a little more about her than I really wanted to know.

"So, why did you leave England?" I asked.

"Well, I can tell you a million reasons, but do you want the truth?"

"The truth," I requested.

"Okay, well in college, I hung out with many progressive minds – you might even say, radical elements – that wanted to see change in England and, for that matter, the world. I was part of many demonstrations, some of which turned angry and violent. Since I am of Arab descent, I was suspected of being anti-English and anti-government. Ultimately, I was asked to leave the country, either nicely or forcibly. I came to the US and settled with my boyfriend, who was also a British Arab. Shortly after getting here, he found someone else and ran off with her and there you have it."

"So, you talked about protests, what sort of things are you referring to? I mean, was it regarding the treatment of immigrants?" I inquired.

"Yes, in part. There were cars overturned, some shops of anti-immigration supporters had their windows broken and their shops burned. General chaos, actually. It wasn't really planned that way, but it turned out much different than expected. I often think that I and many of us that came to the US are being watched."

"Watched?"

I inwardly groaned. Like I needed to hear that another potential date was also being watched by someone or something.

"Yes, there are times when I come home and something in my apartment seems out of place or moved about like someone broke in to look for something."

As dinner finished, she asked me if I had a cigarette.

"No, I don't smoke."

"Not even pot?"

"I am allergic to smoke."

She smiled and shook her head, as if to say, I can't believe you are so square. When dinner was over, I walked her to her car. She stopped and looked at me with an inquisitive expression.

"You're too much of a good boy, aren't you?" she asked.

That was a statement I would hear again a few weeks later. Not waiting for my answer, she turned, got into her car and drove away, never to be seen or heard from again. Who knows, maybe she's still around, in jail, perhaps or even deported for God knows what.

What grape does Fajia remind me of? Wow, she was rough, hard-nosed, not really delicate or sophisticated, per say. I can most relate her to an old world Tannat, which is wine used for blending in France, but also grown in Uruguay. It can be tannic, rough-hewn, lacking character and proper balance. However, a well-produced Tannat can be soft, approachable, wonderfully flavored, spicy and well balanced. She was, however, not the latter.

Sylvia

I met Sylvia on PlentyofFish.com. She was a somewhat attractive, half-Hispanic, half-black woman. Again, since looks are not everything, what she said in her profile about being a cop was very intriguing.

I decided to meet her at the wine bar of choice, The Cork. I got there first. After all, a man must prepare the evening. After the waiter, Bill, had brought the wine and two glasses to the table, she walked through the door. She was a short woman with tightly cropped hair, a tight, black mini skirt, a white top, exposing her adequately sized breasts and a black leather jacket. She saw me straight away and headed toward the table with a big smile.

"Hey Stephen, how are you?"

I shook her hand, which was strong and confident, and she had a seat next to me.

"Nice meeting you," I replied. "Would you like some wine?"

"Sure," she said, still smiling.

"It's Zinfandel."

"As long as it has alcohol in it, I'm fine."

She told me that she was LAPD. And she fit the part. She was kind of sexy and feminine, yet also a little rough and rugged. We talked about wine and what I did for a living, but her profession was much more interesting than mine.

"So, tell me about yourself." I said.

"What do you want to know?"

"Anything at this point."

"My ex-husband and I met when I was on a case."

"Really, he's a cop too?"

"Hell no, he was a criminal. I arrested him for assault and robbery. Guess you could say I have terrible taste in men."

"What did he do?" I asked, trying to mask my surprise.

"What didn't he do? Once, he tied up some blond whore who was known for seducing guys, taking them to her apartment, doing the wild thing, and in the process, making such a racket that the neighbors call to complain. When we got the complaint and headed over there this time, she claimed he was raping her."

"Wow, that's sad." I said, shaking my head.

"Ah, he was a loser. One night, he got drunk, broke into some old man's house and robbed him. He had the balls to steal his electric wheelchair with him still in it."

I choked a bit and tried not to laugh.

"So, that must have been an interesting marriage; cop marries bad guy."

"It was till I shot him... in self-defense, of course," she said before finishing her glass. "He was a crazy bastard, but the sex was fucking amazing."

My next question came out without me even needing to think about it.

"Do you still carry a gun?"

She opened her coat jacket to show me she was packing. An hour went by and she was ripped drunk as she told me more of her police stories.

"So, I taped his hands together around my waist and made him go at it until his tongue was raw."

"How interesting."

"Stephen? Are you a good boy or a bad boy?"

Why do women keep asking me this, I thought to myself. I fumbled for my words for a moment before collecting myself.

"What do you mean? I don't understand."

"Ah, you are a good little boy, aren't you?"

She sticks out her tongue and pretends she's licking me.

"Can we get another bottle of wine?" she asks.

I look at my watch.

"Oh, no, I don't think so. I have a super early morning tomorrow."

She chuckled and let out a burp.

"Am I going to have to take you downtown, Mister?"

"Downtown for what?"

"Refusing to obey the request of a Los Angeles Police Officer," she slurred.

"Well, I really don't need any more wine and neither do you."

"I see... well then, why don't you walk me to my car? There's something I want to show you."

Silvia shows a bit of her breast, the one that happened to be next to her gun.

"No, I'm good."

"What? You don't have the decency to walk me to my car?"

People turned and looked at us.

"No, I didn't say –"

"Walk me to my car. Now!"

"Yes, ma'am," was all I could mutter.

As we left the bar, Bill, the waiter, laughed and gave me a condescending thumbs up. I stared him down. We walked up to the driver's side of her car when she turned to me suddenly.

"Well, it's been interesting. Thanks for meeting me tonight."

Then, she wrapped her strong arms around me and jammed her tongue down my throat. She lip locked me and wouldn't let go. During all this, I peered inside her car and spotted handcuffs and duct tape. Then, I remembered her story about the taped hands and the raw tongue incident. She grabbed my balls and little Elvis and broke off the kiss.

"Average. I'm not sure you could please me anyway."

I felt myself flush.

"Well, then, I guess we're not a match."

She kissed me again and pushed me away.

"You sure can kiss though, too bad. I had such high hopes. Good night, Stephen."

I stood there, stunned, as if I had been hit by a lightning bolt and began to wonder if I should continue to date or just hang it up and become a monk.

And what grape reminds me of Sylvia? A Cabernet. Cab grapes are thicker-skinned, hearty and can grow almost anywhere. However, if grown correctly, the small berries result in more skin to pulp ratio, resulting in a more tannic, deep-colored, bold wine. Now, of course, Cab can be made many different ways, but she reminded me of the big, bold, sometimes tannic and brash Cabs. That grape fits her to a T.

Aracelli

One afternoon, I was having a quick bite at a fast service Mexican restaurant when I spied this petite and very lovely woman having lunch with two other people. I looked at her wedding finger and was pleased to see there was no ring. I, of course, assumed that she was open game. As she approached the trash receptacle with her tray, I walked up to her and said, "I just wanted to say that you are beautiful."

"Wow, no one has said that to me in a long time."

As her eyes met mine, I could sense a sexy, confidence in them.

"You're kidding, right?" I asked. "I mean, I can't believe someone has not told you just how pretty you are."

She looked up at me and smiled.

"Thanks, that's so sweet."

"I'm Stephen," I said, as I reached to take her hand.

"I'm Aracelli."

She glanced down and reached for something in her purse while her friends impatiently waited near the door. I found that it's best not to flirt too long or I run the risk of inadvertently becoming a stalker, so I began to retreat back to my lunch.

"Pleasure meeting you, Aracelli." I said, as I turned to walk back to my table.

"Oh, here's my card."

Her soft hand reached out to grab my arm. I turned back around and took the card, then glanced at it.

"Stone Rock Canyon Apartments. Where is that?"

"Right up the street on McBean near the mall," she said.

According to the card, she was the leasing manager.

"Well, maybe I will have to drop by sometime and see you."

"Please do."

She looked towards the door where her friends were still waiting.

"Well, I had better get back to work; my friends are getting impatient."

"Okay."

"Good meeting you, Stephen."

She and her friends walked out and towards their cars. Moments later, she turned back to look at me with a big smile on her face. There was something about that moment that made my heart race. She was absolutely perfect and I had her card and her number.

Not wanting to seem too anxious or needy, I waited a few days before I called. She seemed excited to hear from me and I asked her if she was free on Friday for dinner. She said that she was and I asked her if she wanted to meet me at the restaurant or if she would like me to pick her up. She said that she felt comfortable with me and asked me to meet her at her office at the apartment complex.

When I arrived, I could see she was sitting at her desk on the phone. I opened the door and walked inside to see one of the people she was with at the restaurant.

He looked up and recognized me instantly.

"Hey, I'm Buddy," he said.

"I'm Stephen. Nice to meet you."

Buddy was a Hispanic man in his mid-forties. He had a grey maintenance shirt with his named stitched on the pocket.

"She'll be done in a second," he said.

I looked at her sitting behind her desk. She waved at me and rolled her eyes at the person and the conversation on the other end of the phone. Aracelli was striking. Her brown skin and dark, short cut hair accented her black dress perfectly.

Finally, the phone call was over and she walked around the desk to meet me. She gave me a hug and a quick once over and then said, "I see you met Buddy."

"Yes."

She said that Buddy was the head of maintenance and he did whatever she asked. Buddy responded sarcastically with, "Yeah, whatever."

She explained that she was waiting for one more call and then we could go. While I waited, I noticed a variety of photos on her desk and one was of her with long hair.

"Wow, this is you?" I said.

She nodded proudly.

"Beautiful, and who is the woman with you?"

"That's my sister," she chimed.

"She's pretty, too."

I sat the picture back down on her desk. The phone rang again and Aracelli answered it. While she was busy, I checked out other pictures of her around the office. One, near where Buddy was sitting, was a stunning portrait of her with long dark hair. I said out loud to Buddy, "Wow's she's hot."

He smiled.

"Yeah, and a pain in the ass, too. You just wait and see."

I was taken aback by his comment, not knowing if he was serious or not. Finally, Aracelli announced she was done and we could go. She grabbed my arm and I escorted her to my car. It was a hot afternoon in the middle of summer and I had the top down on the car.

"Should I put up the top?" I asked, as I placed her into the passenger seat.

"No, it's fine. I love the breeze."

She turned and looked at me. She had a big smile on the face and a gleam in her eyes. I have to tell you, there can be great power and allure in a smile. Once, when I was in Junior High, I was giving a speech and made a mistake. I stopped and was lost for a moment in what I was going to say next. As I paused, I smiled and looked at the class.

"Stop!" my teacher, Ms. Niles, screamed.

I just knew that I was in trouble.

"Did you see what Stephen just did?" she asked the class.

"Yeah, he screwed up," one of the boys said.

The whole class began to chuckle.

"No, he did the thing you should always do when you make a mistake or lose your place in your speech."

I did something right? I remember wondering.

Ms. Niles approached the podium and briefly looked at me, then turned to the class and said, "He smiled, didn't he?"

Many nodded their heads.

"A smile will cover a multitude of sins," she proclaimed.

I felt proud, as if I had accidentally stumbled upon a magic potion. She turned and instructed me to continue and when I was done, I received a loud applause, though most of it came from Ms. Niles.

Back to Aracelli. We were driving to one of my favorite restaurants in town and "Fix You" by Coldplay was playing on my car stereo. She turned to me and, in a serious sort of tone asked, "Is that what you are going to try to do to me?"

I looked at her for a moment.

"Why, do you need fixing?"

And she just smiled that big smile of hers and turned away. I thought it an odd question, but not knowing her sense of humor, I had no reason to suspect anything was wrong with her that needed fixing. Simple flirting, that was all.

Outside on the patio of the restaurant, a band was playing that would become one of my favorite local groups. The Acoustics played cover tunes from the fifties, all the way to current hits. Aracelli and I left our table after dinner to dance and enjoy the beautiful, summer night.

Afterwards, I took her back home. I opened her door and asked her if she wanted me to walk her to her apartment. Before I could even finish asking the question, she placed a passionate, delicious kiss upon my mouth. It was one that I will never forget. She wrapped her arms around me tightly and I kissed her back. She was on fire with passion and I couldn't help but begin to catch fire, as well.

Maybe it was stupid of me, but I didn't want to waste every potential experience with her in one night, so I told her we needed to slow down. She looked at me with eyes full of excitement and passion but agreed to pace herself, just as she launched herself into another kissing frenzy. Finally, we called it a night and I went home with dreams of Aracelli in my head.

Our next encounter took place at an outdoor jazz and blues concert in the mall. I went with my buddy, Asa, to have a glass of wine and listen to music. I had told Aracelli on our first date that I might be there. She said that her mother and sister were going to join her for dinner in the mall and, if they did, she would like me to meet them.

After Asa and I arrived at the concert, I got a call from Aracelli and she said that she and her family were at Rockets, a hamburger place on the outside part of the mall. I asked Asa if he wanted to meet her and he said sure. We walked to the restaurant and Aracelli was outside, waiting for me. She grabbed my hand and instantly introduced me to her family. She was glowing, as if she had found her prince. Her mother, sister and her sister's husband were all very open and welcoming, but since they were late for a movie, they excused themselves and said goodnight. Aracelli came back to give me a kiss and, as she walked away, she yelled, "Call me, I want to see you."

"I will," I screamed back over the crowd.

"Seems like a nice girl," Asa said, with a smile.

That was important to me, as friends can sometimes tell who a person is better than you can, as you are emotionally involved. It's always good to have a friend who can tell it like it is and Asa was just that kind of guy.

I called Aracelli the next day and we decided to get together during the week for a special event at The Cork. The Acoustics, the band we saw a couple of weeks before, were playing. I got to the wine bar as soon as I could after work to claim a table, as the event was sold out. Upon arriving, I was able to snag one of the last, available tables in the place, only because it was right next to the band. No one wanted to be that close and get blasted by the amps and PA system all night, but it was all that was left.

A guy named Cliff sat at the bar near my table and began to chat with me. He was waiting on someone, as well, his brother. As we spoke, he asked me questions about my date – what did she look like, how long had I known her, the usual. Just as I started to respond, she walked through the door. She was wearing a bright red, summer dress. After staring at her for a few moments, I was finally able to mumble, "That's her."

Cliff gave his approval with a simple, "Nice."

I gave her a big hug and a kiss and she sat down at the table. I already had a bottle of Rombauer Zinfandel and two glasses ready. As I poured her wine, I said, "Wow, you look amazing, but I'm sure you know that."

"Thanks, and no, I didn't." she replied, with a smile.

Soon, dinner was served and the band blasted "Brown Eyed Girl" by Van Morrison. Then, one of the most wonderful and erotic moments happened. As the band played, we stared into each other's eyes like two little kids and I fed her every single bite. She never had to lift a finger. It's a little strange to think that serving or feeding someone can be romantic, but it certainly was in this case. I was enthralled with her and she was with me, it seemed.

After dinner, we got up and headed to the dance floor. I am in no way a dancer, but for some reason, somehow, I felt like Fred Astaire when I danced with her. Our moves mirrored each other with such precision and flow that, to me, it felt as if we were of the same body. So, in this beautiful moment, reality came crashing in when least expected.

Behind Aracelli on the dance floor was an Asian woman, whom I had seen many times at the wine bar. She was a fan of the band and was at most of their shows. I was never attracted to her, but we had seen each other quite a bit. While on the dance floor, the Asian woman waved and smiled at me. I, of course, smiled back, which started World War Three. Aracelli caught the look and stomped off the dance floor to the table. Now, maybe wine had something to do with the emotional reaction, but the reality of it was, as I was soon to find out, that Aracelli was a sensitive, jealous soul.

"What happened?" I asked.

"I saw you making eyes at her, Stephen."

"It's not what you imagine," I told her.

"Really? So, you just happened to flirt with her in my presence and expect me to not notice?"

"No, I was not flirting. I know her from being a supporter of the band. She waved hello from the dance floor and I just smiled back. That's it, no harm, no foul."

Aracelli didn't buy it, even though what I said was true. I had zero attraction to this other woman and yet, in my trying to be cordial and nice, I wound up pissing off a woman who I was crazy about.

"I thought you were different. But, I see you're like every other guy. Good night, Stephen."

She grabbed her bag and briskly walked outside. I followed her and pleaded.

"Aracelli, it was nothing. Don't leave."

She kept walking towards her car. Moments later, I stood outside and watched her drive past me and into the night.

I felt so horrible about this silly misunderstanding. I went back inside to my table. As I looked for my keys and hat, a restaurant owner and his wife, who would later become customers and friends of mine, approached me. They went on to say how beautiful Aracelli was and what an amazing couple we made. Little did they know that after tonight, there may not be a couple. I thanked them for their kind words, paid the bill, grabbed my keys and sneaked out the door.

When people first meet each other, I believe a lot of misunderstandings occur because they just don't know each other that well yet, regardless of how seemingly compatible they may be. I chalked this disastrous end to a beautiful evening as just that: a big misunderstanding. So, I decided to try and fix it.

My son, Michael, was spending the week with me, so I told him I would give him a ride to the mall, but he had to go with me to the florist and to drop off flowers to Aracelli first.

"So, you really pissed her off, huh, Dad?" Michael asked, with typical teenager sarcasm.

"Yeah, I guess you could say that. Enough to pay for a dozen, red roses."

We drove up to her office and I walked inside with the huge bouquet of flowers. Aracelli saw me and the look on her face was not one of joy and happiness. I handed her the roses and sighed.

"I don't know how things got so messy last night," I began. "But, I want you to know, I am not interested in anyone but you."

I paused as she thought about what I was saying. I smiled, as I remembered the wisdom I learned from my teacher: A smile can cover a multitude of sins. I asked her for forgiveness and if she would go out with me again.

"Well, the roses are pretty and you seem to be sincere. I guess we could try it again."

"Great!" I said excitedly.

She looked out the window and into my car.

"Who's that?"

"My son, Michael, I'm taking him to the mall."

"He's cute."

"Would you like to come up to my house for dinner and some of my wine this weekend?" I asked.

"Sure, but can I trust you?"

She smiled devilishly.

"Yes, absolutely. I will be a gentleman."

"Let me know what time."

She walked away, glancing back at me with a seductive look on her face. I could barely handle it, so I got the heck out of there and back into my car.

"Did it work?" Michael asked.

"Like a charm."

As we drove away, I was thinking about how happy I was she agreed to see me again. It was hard to think of anything else.

So, the weekend came and I had everything prepared for Aracelli to dine at my home. I made rib eye steaks with peppercorn sauce and garlic mashed potatoes and asparagus on the side. I also had two bottles of my Syrah from 2003 ready to roll.

As she drove up the long, rough dirt road to my house, I was jumping with excitement. I had not felt that way since first meeting Mary years before. My stomach was in knots, so I took a few long, deep breaths.

Finally, she arrived at my door, where she was immediately greeted by my little dog, Sammy. As she stepped through the door, she immediately said, "What a cute dog! What's his name?"

"Ah, that's Sammy."

She kneeled down and gave him a kiss on the head and, to be honest, I was hoping she might give me one, as well. Sure enough, she stood up, walked in the door, wrapped her arms around me and placed a passionate kiss on my mouth. She felt so amazing in my arms. It was as if her small petite body was made for me. Custom fit by God and the universe.

After a moment of passionate kisses, I showed her around the house. My home is not a show place, by any means, nor is it grand in size or quality of furnishings, but there is a certain vibe to my old 1954 home that resonates with so many people. Interestingly enough, it is the same age as me, so I feel like it somehow knows me, and I, it. When Mary lived here, she adorned the walls with many of her wonderful murals and helped create this warm, sunny and positive environment.

I had Frank Sinatra and Dean Martin music playing in the background, and the lights turned down to create a warm and romantic atmosphere.

"Great place, I like it. It makes me feel comfortable." she said, as she looked around.

"I'm glad you feel comfortable. Hey, tell me what you think of this wine," I said, handing her a glass.

She swirled it in the glass and took a sniff and then a sip.

"Wonderful, where's it from?"

"It's my Syrah from Santa Maria."

"It's really good."

Some women are quite impressed if a man can cook or make and repair things, but I have found that they seemed really intrigued when a man is a wine maker. Part of the sex and allure of the vine, I suppose.

Aracelli was impressed enough to wrap her arms around me once more and place small, gentle kisses all around my face. When she finished lavishing me with kisses, I took a moment to catch my breath before I got started cooking the steak.

She sat at the island in the kitchen and watched me cook. I caught her looking at me time to time with what I hope could only be described as her thinking, "I like this guy."

When the steaks were done, we transported the plates, wine and glasses out to the patio, where an absolutely perfect summer evening awaited. We ate, drank and talked about anything and everything. We spoke about our families and where we grew up. What she told me about her past, however, made my life seem like it had belonged to the Royal Family.

Like so many people, her parents split up when she and her sister were young. Her mother was Mexican and her father Lebanese, which explained her unique and striking look. Her father stayed in Mexico, while her mother came to California with their two young daughters, seeking work and a new life. Aracelli was left alone most of the time with her little sister, as her mother worked every job imaginable to make a living for the three of them.

"I despised my mom," she said, sadly.

"Why?"

"She was rarely there for us. She was always working or busy and my sister and I would roam the streets, hanging out with all the wrong people."

"My God, I'm sorry to hear that. Have you forgiven her?"

"Why would I forgive her?" she asked, angrily.

"For clarity and resolve, to start. Anger is poison to your well-being and you must forgive her, even if you don't forget what she did."

She looked down at her plate, then back at me.

"You're right. I know she did the best she knew how, but she wasn't there for us."

"Where is your father and do you ever hear from him?" I asked.

"He's still in Mexico. The last time I saw him, I was 19. I drove to see him in Mexico and when I was there, he asked me to take a package to a friend in Los Angeles for him. I put the package in the glove box of my car and headed back to LA. At the border, they searched my car, but for some weird reason, they never looked in the glove box. When I got home, I took the package to my dad's friend and it was $100,000 in cash for some drug deal. My father used me, his daughter, as a mule to complete a drug transaction. I refused to talk to that son of a bitch ever again," she said, with tears in her eyes.

All I could do was sit there in awe. I tried to say something, but the only thing that came out was a feeble apology.

"Aracelli, I am so sorry. I have a daughter and son and I never could imagine doing that to them."

There was a long pause. Aracelli wanted to talk more about her life and, somehow, I was the perfect person to hear it. I let her continue on without interruption.

"My sister and I were both molested by uncles and gang members when we were younger, but we never got into trouble or drugs, even though we were surrounded by both. I was able to move away from my mother's care, if you could call it that, and into my own place when I was around 16. I have pretty much raised myself and my sister."

"How did you cope with all that chaos?"

"Prozac."

I got up, walked around to her and gave her a warm and consoling hug as she sat in her chair. I took her hand and we walked over to the hammock bed and lay down together. No sex, not even the idea of it. Just two spirits bonding and sharing a moment in time. She felt so good to me with her back to my chest, spooned up against me and me holding her in my arms. Our breathing became one and I could smell the alluring essence of her skin and hair. This was so good, so right.

An hour or so of bliss passed and she asked if she could use the bathroom. I told her sure and took her into the house. I pointed to the guest bathroom down the hallway.

"Is there another one?" she asked.

"Yes, one in my master bedroom."

"Show me!"

She grabbed my hand and I took her to my bedroom and once inside, I pointed to the door to the restroom. However, she had no intent of using it. She started taking off my shirt as she kissed my face. I told her no, but she was not listening. She unbuttoned my pants and pulled them down. Again, I tried to stop her.

"Aracelli, slow down."

In a flash, she had me undressed and at full attention and she began taking off her clothes. I'm no prude and I was definitely interested, but I was concerned about the rapid pace that things were going. Whatever happened to courtship and a little mystery?

I had to admit she had a beautiful body – lovely, brown skin and a perfectly round ass. Her legs were nicely shaped and her cupcake size breasts were enticing. She gave me a look and said, "Come and make love to me."

She pulled me on top of her and, without any foreplay, other than her passionate kisses, she grabbed my ass and repeated, "Make love to me."

About three or four minutes in, she suddenly screamed, "NO!"

She kicked me off of her and I went flying to the end of the bed. She pushed herself up against the headboard, crossed her legs and wrapped her arms around the top of her legs. She had this angry, hurt look on her face.

"What happened? Are you okay?" I asked, breathing heavily.

She only stared at me.

"Aracelli, what just happened?"

She reached out and wrapped her arms around my shoulders and, with force, pulled me back on top of her. I was confused, but I still wanted to share this moment with her, so I got back into it. She was thrusting her hips and moaning in ecstasy until she again screamed, "NO!"

She kicked me off of her again. Again, I wound up at the foot of the bed and she sat back in the same position as before. I was not only confused, but also a little upset and worried.

"Aracelli, what the hell is going on?"

She just stared at me with that angry, hurt look.

"Listen, if you want to role play, I'm OK with it, but just let me know, so I can also play along."

She continued to stare a hole in me. Now, I was starting to sense that there is a real problem here. I didn't want to play this game anymore, so I tucked myself into bed on the other side of her. Moments later, she sat up and glared at me.

"What just happened?" I asked.

"You wouldn't understand."

"Try me; I'm a pretty open-minded guy."

She said nothing and then, I remembered something.

"Did you forget your Prozac?" asked.

She glared at me, then took a deep breath and changed the subject.

"Do you have any Vicodin?" she asked.

Having had many knee surgeries, I had some around for when my pain got a little out of hand. I leaned over to the nightstand and pulled out a little vial and gave it to her. She pulled the top off the jar and looked in.

"Would you like some?"

"No! Do you think I need this stuff? Are you trying to get me fucked up?" she yelled at me, with a psychotic look in her eyes.

I had enough of this crazy behavior and I put the vial back into the nightstand and asked her to get dressed and leave my home. She got up and started putting her clothes on. In the meantime, I was disappointed and concerned that she had not only come unglued, but was having a complete meltdown. Once dressed, she asked, "Are you going to walk me to my car?"

"Nope, you know where you parked it."

She grabbed her purse and before leaving, screamed her final words in my presence.

"Fuck you!"

I heard the car engine start when I suddenly remembered how much she liked Sammy. I ran around the house naked, looking for the little rat, in fear she had stolen him. But, there he was, in the living room, asleep. I picked him up, ran to the window and watched her drive down the road in the middle of the night. Years later, that was still one of the oddest encounters I have ever been through. It's a shame, really. With all the synergy and chemistry that we seemed to share, it's sad that it would all turn out this way.

About four months later, my house was broken into. Well, not really broken into, as I always left the back door unlocked for the housecleaner and gardener, but invaded, nonetheless. When I got home from work one day, the back door was ajar and Sammy and another dog I was watching were gone.

I walked into the house, sensing someone had violated my space. The big screen TV was still there and so was the stereo and my wine collection. But, the cabinets in the kitchen and all the drawers in my bedroom dressers and nightstands were open and torn through like a hurricane had hit them. In the master bath, the medicine cabinets were thrown open and the contents knocked about.

Noticeably gone was my laptop, which had contained all the scripts I had written, along with my camera and, guess what else, my little vial of Vicodin.

I called the sheriff's department right away. They sent an officer to fingerprint the house, but came up with two unidentifiable fingerprints. The detective said it seemed like the work of some kids looking for drugs. I did not buy his explanation for the robbery. If the culprit had been a couple of kids, they would have taken some of my musical instruments, as well. My bass and acoustic guitars were worth more than anything else they took and were easy to steal and carry. The sheriff told me once that they saw the contents of the house, they would be back.

I immediately called Brinks and ordered a security system. Somehow, my private little oasis had come under attack. Now, I could no longer have the security and peace of mind I once thought was mine.

The kicker came a few days after the robbery. I got a call from Rosa, Enrique's wife.

"Señor Stephen, I was driving past your house and saw you got lucky last night," Rosa teased in her cute, broken English.

"What do you mean?"

"Well, me see a girl – she pretty – in a white car pulling out of your road and onto the highway. I figure you and she have a good weekend together," she said.

"What did she look like?"

"I don't know for sure, as she was in front of me, but she have dark, short brown hair and was driving a little, white car."

All of her descriptions fit Aracelli.

"Did you follow her? Did you see where she went?"

"She turn left on Soledad and I went right, so I'm not sure."

I thanked her, but told her that I did not have anyone over for the weekend and that whomever she saw might have been the one that robbed me. Poor Rosa freaked out when she realized that maybe this person was the guilty party.

I suspected Aracelli more than ever, not only because of the matching descriptions of her and her car, but also because she had Mondays off and she knew that I left work around eight every morning. She knew where the Vicodin was, that I was writing scripts and that Sammy wouldn't bite her if she came in the house. I was never able to prove anything, but in my heart, I believe she robbed me. Guess it was payback for rejecting her strange behavior and making her walk herself back to her car.

Aracelli is now, from what I hear, with the love of her life. I can only pray that she has broken the shackles of her sad, lonely past and is at peace with it. Or, more than likely, found a fool willing to deal with her strange, mercurial behavior. Whatever the case, I pray that she has found herself along the path to self-realization and is creating the life that she deserves.

Her grape? Viognier. Soft, thin-skinned and some-times hard to grow, much like a Pinot Noir. However, as difficult as they are to get right, they provide a lovely, almost sexy flower and honeysuckle nuance. It is a delicate, sensual, very flavorful wine, and a great choice instead of a Chardonnay or Sauvignon Blanc.

Aracelli was like this wine – soft, sexy and yet, difficult to handle and understand.

The Two Tracy's

After the chaos of those short-lived relationships, I wanted anyone who seemed stable and normal. Of course, no guy wants a normal, boring woman, but I just wanted some relief from the daredevil, high wire relationships I had so far encountered.

I went out with Tracy #1 for only one date. She was a white woman with blonde hair and pretty, blue eyes in her late 30's. She was nice, but there was absolutely zero chemistry between us. As insignificant as the date was, the ride home was quite interesting as I was pulled over at a CHP checkpoint near my house. We had split one bottle of wine over a three-hour period. That equated to two glasses each or one every hour and a half.

Trying to make something out of nothing, the Smoky Bear hat little Nazi made me pull over in the lot of a convenience store. There, he made me get out of the car and began his interrogation.

"How much did you have to drink, sir?"

I then repeated what I had already told him.

"I shared a bottle of wine with a friend."

"You drank a bottle of wine!"

"No, I shared a bottle of wine with a date," I politely corrected him.

He then began to ask a series of totally unneeded, worthless and yet, personal questions.

"What did you have for breakfast?"

"A protein shake."

"Do you have any injuries?"

"Well, I had four surgeries on my left knee."

"Does it hurt?"

"Yes, constantly."

"What did you have for dinner tonight? What is your weight? How far do you live from here? What do you do for a living? Who do you work for?"

After I answered all of his questions, he instructed me to do a field sobriety test. He had me touch my nose with my outstretched arms and fingers, walk a straight line, count forward and backwards from 100 and then, stand on one foot with my arm extended out like a bird.

When I stood on my injured left knee, I lost my balance.

"Why are you wobbling?"

I was a little miffed that he already forgot the answer to his own question.

"This is the knee I had surgery on four times," I reminded him.

"Well, you passed all the exercises, but I still want to do a Breathalyzer on you."

Are you serious? I thought to myself. All of this over two glasses of wine in three hours? He and his CHP pal administered the test and when it was done, he instructed me to go back and sit in my car. I did as told.

A few moments later, he came over to me and handed me my license back.

"Guess what, you're not inebriated."

I smiled.

"I know I'm not and I could have saved you all this time."

"Get out of here, now!" he shouted, while pointing down the road.

I left thinking that they were not so interested in catching someone drunk as they were with torturing people and finding a reason to give them a ticket and raise money for the state.

A few weeks later, my sister-in-law, Joy, called to say she wanted to hook me up with someone she knew from the hair salon she went to in Studio City. This was perfect because I wanted to find a date for a company awards ceremony and dance that was coming up in a few weeks. That's when I met Tracy #2.

She was a forty-year-old black woman who taught third grade in Pasadena. I talked to her a couple of times on the phone and I could tell a couple of things right off the bat. First, she was very energetic and could talk my ear off. Secondly, she spoke differently, both in voice and speech. She later told me that she was from Detroit, so that explained her accent, but she also spoke what some might call, "Black American slang" or "Ebonics."

I picked her up at her place in Glendale for the long trek and overnight stay in Ventura for the awards ceremony. The fact that she trusted me that much to stay overnight with me was interesting. I met her at her door and she invited me in. As I had never seen a picture of her, I was surprised to see that she was pretty and had a sweet smile and seemed very warm. She was around five feet four inches tall and, from what I could tell, had a tight, wound, little frame and nice skin. It's funny how much a man's eye can scan and process in a very short amount of time.

She said that she needed a few moments to finish getting ready and asked if I wanted a glass of wine. I of course, said sure.

"The glasses and wine be on the counter," she said.

I helped myself to some Merlot – yep, a woman's wine – and had a seat in her living room. Her place was small, but nicely decorated. You could sense she was very clean and organized. Moments later, she appeared in a black dress.

"Wow, you look great," I said.

"You look great in your suit, as well."

After a short moment of silence, she said that she was ready to go.

"Well then, let's hit the road."

She grabbed her purse, a small overnight case and out the door we went.

Now, one thing was already presenting itself as a challenge to me. I am extremely sensitive to certain aromas and I think she may have spilled a whole bottle of perfume on herself. It was a very over-the-top, cloying perfume at that.

Once we got in the car, the top and windows immediately came down so I could breathe. I asked if she was okay with it, as having experienced black women before, they are extremely concerned about their hair. With the top down and hitting 65, miles per hour they could start out with a well-coifed hair do, only to have it look like Buckwheat from the "Little Rascals" once we reached our destination. No woman wants to look like Buckwheat, at least not to my knowledge.

We spoke about a few things on the way – the lousy traffic, poor pay for teachers and the fact that many of the kids in her classroom were Hispanic and the parents of these kids didn't speak a lick of English. She said this made teaching the kids difficult, as the parents could not help them with homework.

"I feel sorry for some of these kids. They need parents to be involved and they just ain't."

We arrived at the hotel and were late. We quickly checked in and took the bags to our room before heading back down to the main meeting area for dinner and awards. After finding my group and our two tables, Tracy and I had a seat. We had pre-registered what we were going to eat and so within a few minutes, dinner was served.

Just as I was starting to relax and get into the party mood, my phone rang. It was my wine bar, The Cork, and the manager, Betty, was beyond pissed off.

"Stephen, we have a problem."

"And what is that?"

"We have no sea bass and I understand it's your fault."

"What do you mean, it's my fault?"

"Chef Fred says you picked up one case and never delivered another and we are completely out," she said, beginning to get louder.

"Listen, you had two cases and Fred wanted to return one because he over-ordered, so there should still be a case there."

"Well, there is not and he told me you were supposed to bring a case!"

"Betty, why would I bring a case if he's returning one?"

"I don't care how things got messed up; you need to bring us a case right away!" she screamed.

"I can't because I am out of town at a Super Foods overnight function and the warehouse is closed until Monday."

"Well, we are going to have to make some changes, as you are not providing the type of service we need here."

"Betty, I always bust my ass for you, but this is not my mistake, nor can I do anything about it at nine o'clock on a Friday night. If you want to fire me, do so, but your new chef messed up, not me, and I won't take the rap for it."

She got so mad that she hung up on me.

I was muttering to myself as I walked back to the table. I sat down and I was sure that everyone could see the red in my eyes and the stress in my face. They began to ask me if I was okay.

"No, but I will be soon," I replied, as I chugged my glass of wine.

Thank God for open bars. The night got better, as I was presented with a $4 million sales mark award and the DJ cranked up the music. Tracy and I danced, drank and had a good time. She was easy to be with and that really helped, being pissed off like I was.

Once our partying was over, we headed back to the room and undressed. I stripped down to underwear and a t-shirt. She looked like an innocent, little girl in her matching red pajamas. We went to bed with no hugging or kissing and no hanky-panky, just some much needed sleep.

The next morning, we got up and took a long walk on the beach before joining everyone else for breakfast. As we packed up our things to head back home, I looked at Tracy and thought about the things I liked about her. Even her overuse of perfume and use of slang didn't really bother me enough to never want to see her again. In fact, I invited her to my house a week later for dinner.

We slept together, but again, there was no hanky-panky. We did kiss a little this time, but that was all. I held her as she slept.

When we woke up, we hung out in bed talking and she had me in stitches with her stories and the way she told them with such energy and excitement.

"My girlfreeeeeind, she got this old man name Curtis and he be always doin shit to her."

"Like what?" I asked.

"He be an airplane pilot and he is old and nasty. Yet, she be with him cause he buys her things and takes her all over the world."

"That doesn't sound too awful."

"Yeah, but he be married and he won't get no divorce, so my friend is upset."

"I can see that."

"Yeah, and he even put my friend up in a townhouse, got her a car and everything, but his sorry ass won't marry her."

"Can I tell you something?" I asked.

"Yeah."

"Why should he? He has the perfect life. A wife at home, a mistress he can enjoy when he can and a jet-set lifestyle. And, she's not doing too badly, either, really. It sounds like he treats her well."

"Yeah, but she wants him to herself and she ain't getting that."

"Be careful what you wish for. Enjoy what you have; it may be better than what you want."

"You may be right, I'm gonna tell her that."

Tracy was fun, so I asked her to go up to Santa Ynez wine country with me. We hit my favorite places, like Zaca Mesa, Kohler, Curtis, Foxen, Melville, Sanford and a few others. Again, Tracy was just easy to be around. There were no psychological breakdowns, traumas or arguments. She was easy-going, laughed often and seemed to love my company.

As the day wound down, we went to my chosen place to eat, Firestone Brewery. I like to sit at the bar that surrounds the kitchen and watch the chefs do their thing because they are damn good at it. Normally, I order the seared ahi tuna that is to die for, but that night, I felt like a hamburger. Tracy ordered the tuna and loved it while I felt more like a carnivore and destroyed my half pound Angus burger. We shared a bottle of wine for dinner and then, drove the twenty minutes to the motel.

Upon arriving at the Quality Motel in beautiful Lompoc, we quickly unpacked, brushed our teeth and headed to bed. We held each other as we watched a movie, but again, nothing more. Actually, she seemed more open to something happening, but I was starting to feel sick, so much so that my stomach was bloated and stirring like a cement mixer. I excused myself about five times using the toilet and was still feeling like crap, (pun intended). I knew there was a Jacuzzi downstairs near the pool and I thought that maybe the hot, swirling water might relieve my pain. I asked her if she wanted to go with me.

"Nah, I think I'll finish watching this movie," she replied.

"Okay, I'll be back in a little."

The Jacuzzi felt wonderful and I even swam a few laps in the pool to try to work off the alcohol and the lethargic, bloated feeling that possessed me. It didn't work. I went back up to the room feeling as horrible as ever. I tried to sleep, but I was up all night visiting the porcelain

God. Tracy also was started feeling sick and I remembered that she had a few of bites of my burger. I don't believe we got any sleep and unfortunately, it wasn't because of the expected reason. Turns out, we had a slight, yet effective case of food poisoning.

The next day, we felt a little better. We went wine tasting, but took it easy. We had lunch in Solvang, and then headed home. Since she had driven up to my house, I needed to allow her time to drive back about 45 minutes to her place in Glendale. Once we got back, she told me how much she enjoyed the weekend and she gave me a kiss before getting into her car.

A few weeks later, she came over to my house for dinner and a sleepover. This time, things went a little further. She slept in only her bra and panties and, for the first time, I could see what a solid, attractive body she possessed. We kissed and did everything but make love.

In the morning, I felt her lying next to me and I planted kisses on her forehead. During the night, she had removed her bra and her breasts were not only perfectly shaped, but her nipples, by virtue of my forehead kisses, stood up like pencil erasers. I placed a kiss on both breasts and she moaned. We kissed some more and she sat up on her knees in bed and held me close to her in the same position. I could feel her breasts and nipples pressed against me, as well as her pulse beating in her neck. I was hard as a rocket and it was ready to take off, but we stopped there. As hard as it was (pun intended), we didn't go any further. Kissing her full juicy lips and feeling her body next to me was more than enough, though.

I was amazed at how well this woman knew how to pace things, unlike the others I had been with who almost raped me after a few dates. There was something kind of cool about waiting that made the act even more intriguing.

Christmas was approaching and she was going back to Michigan to see her parents. I took her out before she left to a quaint, French restaurant near her home. She asked me to stay the night with her and I accepted. We began making out and then, things finally went where we had wanted to go, but never did. She asked me to make love to her.

Trust me, I was ready and willing, and I tried, but I couldn't get it in. It sounds weird that I couldn't fit my not-so-large member inside a forty-year-old woman, but I couldn't. It was like trying to fit a baseball bat through a wire fence. It went in little, but not all the way. I looked at her and she knew what my question was going to be.

"Are you really that tight?" I asked.

"Baby, ain't anybody been up in here in a long, long time and I ain't had any kids, so it is what it is. Here, let me get something."

She got up and went to her overnight bag. Moments later, she returned with a tube of KY jelly. I tried again and was able to "break on through to the other side", as the Doors song would say, but then it happened. She was still so tight, little Elvis could only hold out for about two minutes before he gave up the ghost. I was embarrassed and felt like I had let her down. This had never happened to me this quickly in my adult life. I could usually hang in there for quite a while, but this was ridiculous. I apologized and she told me not to worry. I explained that I could do better and she told me it was okay. She knew she was tight and that we would try again after she got back from Michigan.

She left the next day and she would call me many times while there. For some reason that I still can't comprehend, I just didn't care. Not to be rude, but I liked her and we had good physical chemistry together, but something still did not motivate me to get excited about her or us. Maybe it was because I didn't feel a deep spiritual or mental connection with her.

While away, we talked a few times on the phone and she sent me e-mails, saying how much she was starting to like me. She even sent me flowers, but I felt guilty about not feeling the same way and so I broke it off. I told her my ex-girlfriend had come back to me and I felt I needed to give it a shot. For a long period of time, I felt horrible for being a coward and not telling her the truth.

She got back into town and sent me an e-mail about how much she enjoyed being with me and how she wished me happiness. Looking back, I might have messed up a good thing. I realize now that I had been judging her against Mary and the relationship we had, which was unfair. I also was a little intimidated by her ability to challenge my manhood. The question I had to ask myself after Tracy was, "What am I really looking for?"

Tracy #2 is like Sangiovese aka Chianti. Light and fruity, yet tasty and easy to drink. Unless this grape is made incorrectly, it will yield a simple, but sometimes, complex, fruit-forward wine that can be served with meals or simply drank alone. It's a wine that few would have an issue with. That was Tracy.

Janice

I met Janice on the internet through Match.com. She was a voluptuous, blonde woman with all the right things in all the right places. She had a Marilyn Monroe look to her, complete with a beauty mark on her left cheek. We had chatted a few times on instant messenger and agreed to meet at The Cork.

I arrived at the wine bar and Bill, the waiter, came by to see if I needed anything.

"Not yet," I replied.

"Another hot date?"

"Yep."

"What's her name?"

For a second, I was stumped. I had met so many women that I had forgotten. Just then, she entered the room and for the love of God, I couldn't remember her name.

"Shit, I can't remember. Think, damn it." I muttered to myself in front of Bill. She recognized me and waved as she approached the table.

"Stephen?"

"Ah... Yes. Hey, how are you? This is Bill and Bill, this is..."

"Janice. I'm Janice."

She smiled at Bill and glared at me for forgetting her name. I quickly tried to cover up my faux pas.

"I was going to say that, but I was so struck by your beauty that I forgot. Funny, huh?" I eeked out.

"Yeah, real funny. This is a cool place," she noted, looking around.

"Yes, it is. So, what kind of wine do you like?"

"Oh, I only drink white wine. Red gives me a headache."

"White, it is."

I turned to Bill, who was staring at her chest.

"Bill, would you get Janice a chardonnay and me a glass of–"

"Let me guess, Zinfandel." Bill interrupted, while still enamored with her breasts.

"Yes, of course."

Bill slowly and reluctantly left the table.

"So, you come here a lot?" Janice asked.

"It's my favorite hangout and one of my accounts."

"What do you do?"

She stared at me with her large, brown eyes. They were so sensual and misty that I had to take a moment before I could answer.

"I sell food and supplies to restaurants."

"And, do you like it?"

"I do. I mean, sometimes it's tough because some customers can be so difficult, but you have to learn to deal with their psychotic personalities."

Bill arrived with the wine.

"And, what do you do for a living?" I asked.

"I work in the service industry, too," she stated, with a sultry smile.

"Food, beverage, hotel?"

"Airlines, I'm a flight attendant."

"Really? So, in all of your travels, what is your favorite place?"

She smiled like the Cheshire cat and, with a gleam in her eye, she said nothing and chose to leave me in mystery. About three hours later, she showed me that favorite place of hers – her apartment.

She had me tie her hands to the bed post and, as she lay there, nude, squirming and begging me to take her, I fumbled around, trying to put on a condom. Having been fixed and primarily with two women in my prior 26 years of captivity, er, marriage, I was not used to, nor liked those little bastards. As thumping music played on her iPod and stereo, I messed around, trying to work the condom onto little Elvis.

"Hurry up." she demanded.

"I'm trying!"

"Don't you know how to put a condom on?"

"Yes. I've just not had to wear one for a long, long time."

"Come here, I'll put it on for you."

"No, I can do it."

Finally, it was on and ready for action. I started to kiss her, but she was more interested in little Elvis than the intimate details of a kiss.

"Put it in!" she screamed.

I did as I was told.

"Mm... Yes, harder. Oh God yes, harder!" she squealed with delight.

Then, she got louder and louder.

"Do me, you animal!"

I was aware we were in a building with many tenants and surely, someone would hear her screaming.

"Shush, please be quiet," I begged.

"Screw you. Screw me. Give it all you got, big boy!"

The bed was making loud, creaking noises and head-board was pounding the wall. All of a sudden, a neighbor next door started beating on the wall.

"For the love of God, be quiet!"

"Fuck you," Janice yelled back.

I got freaked out at the exchange and stopped for a moment.

"What are you doing? Get back to work," she instructed.

"I think maybe I should go." I said, meekly.

That was not the answer she wanted to hear and she tightened her legs around my waist like a chain and squeezed the air right out of me. I gasped for breath and she looked me in the eyes and said, threateningly, "You're not going anywhere!"

I went back to work and it felt like just that. Soon, she was again screaming at the top of her lungs.

"Oh, my God! Yes! Yes! Harder! Harder!"

The neighbor banged on the wall again and screamed, "Is this hard enough?"

"Kiss my ass," Janice shouted back.

Scared and shocked, I took my hand and covered her mouth while I pleaded with her to stop screaming.

"Sssh. Please keep it down." She bit my hand and this time, I screamed, "Shit! That hurt!"

"Now, make me hurt, baby. Make me hurt, big boy. Oh God."

"That's it! I called the cops!" the neighbor exclaimed from the other side of the wall.

Then, it hit me. I flashed back to what Sylvia, the cop who told me about a blonde whore, as she called her, who seduced guys and when they had sex, would scream and moan and then, claim she was being raped when the cops arrived. I jumped up like I was on fire and put on my clothes.

"Where the hell are you going?" she asked.

"I'm out of here," I said, as I put on my shoes.

"You can't. You have a job to do."

"Sorry, I quit."

As I opened her door, I looked each way down the hall to see if anyone was watching.

"Hey, are you going to untie me?"

I looked back at her and said, "No, I'm not, but nice meeting you."

I closed the door and, as quietly as I could, briskly walked down the hallway. I could still hear her and the neighbor screaming at each other as I headed down the stairs.

"Cops are on the way," the neighbor announced.

I got to the front of her building and quickly snuck away, like a thief into the night. As I got to my car and unlocked the door, I saw a police car slowly pulling up to her building. I slid into the driver's seat and watched them get out and walk towards the front door of the apartment complex. I did a double take and saw that one of the cops looked like Sylvia.

Holy crap, I said to myself.

I waited anxiously for them to go inside. Once they were gone, I took a deep breath and slowly drove away. That night, I said many prayers and meditated my ass off.

Janice was like a Sauvignon Blanc. A grape that can be made into many different styles of wine, but most often is grassy, even weedy, with a color of straw that matched her hair. It's a wine that many people love or hate and nothing to me tastes similar to it. It can be acidic and wild in flavor or tame and flat. Just try a California versus New Zealand or Australia Sauvignon Blanc and you will get what I am saying.

Gloria

One night, I was at my buddy, Enrique's, who owns La Cuisine, and he and my friend, Rusty, were talking about my adventures in dating. I had just recapped the Janice scenario.

"Sounds like a real psycho," Rusty said.

"I would never date anyone off the internet." Enrique proclaimed.

"Well, not all the nuts in the world are from the internet. Many I have met in person," I explained.

"Why don't you do things you love and maybe you'll meet someone there?" Enrique suggested. "You know, wine clubs, wine tasting fund-raisers, community service organizations."

"What about self-improvement seminars, retreats or even new-age churches. You're into that spiritual stuff. Check it out, you never know," Rusty added.

In Santa Clarita, there are not really any churches that are open to my spiritual beliefs. I tend to favor meditation over group recited prayer and peace and tranquility over a fire and brimstone sermon. I grew up Southern Baptist and I never agreed with, nor believed the scare tactics that all-knowing God was a judging, angry and punishing being. I believe God gave us free will and the ability to seek happiness in whatever form that may be. Most of the churches where I live tend to be much like what I experienced as a child: dogmatic and swayed to that religion's point of view. To me, religion can be a great barrier to understanding each other and to the communion with God, as it becomes not a personal relationship, but one created by the middle man, the church. That's what was attractive about the Agape in Culver City. It was open to all spiritual beliefs and seemed to be a dogma-free zone.

As I arrived at Agape, I was blown away by the eclectic mix of ethnicities, cultures and ages. It seemed to be a church for all people. Once inside, the place was packed to the rafters. I found a seat far in back of the church. I immediately liked the feel of the place and the energy of it. Then, the minister spoke.

"May we now take a few moments of silence in meditation to thank our Creator for all the challenges, blessings and love that we have in our lives?"

He bowed his head and the congregation meditated in complete silence. I let my mind wander, as it usually does when meditating. I used to feel like I wasn't concentrating enough, but that's what you are supposed to do. If a thought enters your mind, allow it to leave without much consternation. Should you give the thought your attention, it will linger longer.

Once the meditation was over, I opened my eyes to see a fit, cute, black woman in front of me to my right. I don't know if it was my energy or the fact that I was staring a hole through her, but she opened her eyes and looked at me. She smiled and I returned the smile.

After the service, I walked up to her.

"It's wonderful that the minister does not beat you to death with dogma."

"That's one of the reasons I come here. Not to mention, all the beautiful souls that fill this place," she replied.

Outside, we continued to walk together in silence among the huge crowd of people. Then, she turned and looked at me.

"I'm Gloria," she said, strongly shaking my hand.

"Nice meeting you, Gloria, I'm Stephen."

We wound up talking for a while and exchanged numbers.

A few weeks after meeting her, I was scheduled to go up north to Sonoma and Napa wine country with friends Rusty and Anna. I would be revisiting the scene of my last miserable days with Mary. We were having dinner and wine at their home when Anna looked at me and said, "Rusty and I are so looking forward to our trip to Sonoma. So, who are you going to take with you?"

"I'm not sure. I met a woman in church the other day."

"You went to church?" Rusty asked, with a Cheshire cat grin on his face.

"Yeah, you were the one that suggested it, remember?"

Rusty laughed and nodded his head.

"She's into many of the same things I am. Wine, food, the arts, spiritual books and she's pretty," I continued.

"What's her name?" Anna asked.

"Gloria."

"What about taking her?"

"I don't know all that much about her to spend the whole three days together."

"Sounds like you have a few things in common, though. Ask her," Anna urged.

Rusty shook his head in agreement.

The next day, I called her and she instantly accepted my offer. I was just praying this would not be a fiasco like the trip before with Mary.

We got up to the Sonoma area on a Friday morning. I planned the trip with the purpose to visit as many wineries as possible, but keep the trip low-key and unhurried. I also had a friend from a large wine distribution company who arranged tours and special tastings at a few of the wineries.

The first stop was, of course, Buena Vista, where I was a cellar member and received free tasting. We started with a Sauvignon Blanc.

"Has a perfect balance of acidity and fruit. Very clean," I reported.

We all took a swirl and then, a sip.

"There's a little citrus and pear to it, as well," Anna added.

She turned to Rusty and asked, "What do you think?"

"I don't know. It tastes good... so I drink it."

Gloria cracked up and spit half her wine out over the bar. Laughing and choking on her wine, she giggled, "I was going to say the same thing. I guess Rusty and I don't have the same ability to taste wine as you two."

"Wine is simply an education of the senses. It just takes practice to understand and appreciate the nuance of each particular grape and the way it's made," I explained.

Gloria swirled and sniffed her glass.

"I don't know. I love wine, but I can't describe it. I think some people just have better palates."

As we enjoyed the wine, Anna, began to ask questions of my new friend.

"So, do you mind me asking how old you are?" Anna inquired.

"51," Gloria proudly stated.

"No way, you look amazing."

"Thank you."

"How do you do it? I mean, you have the body of a 30-year-old woman."

"I do Yoga two hours a day, seven days a week."

"Wow," Anna said, in awe.

We visited many other fabulous wineries before having dinner. Once we got back to the motel, we got the keys to our rooms, and said good night. After all, wine tasting is hard, tiring work. We made plans the next morning to have breakfast at the motel and head out for more wine tasting adventures.

Gloria and I slid into the room and put our bags on the floor.

"I'm going to clean up a bit. I'll be right back," she said.

I changed into a t-shirt and boxers and brushed my teeth at the sink. I could hear her humming and singing in the shower and then, she surprised me by ripping a fart. I almost choked on my toothpaste. I left the bathroom and walked over to the TV, turned it on and plopped down onto the bed. Within seconds, it seemed, I was asleep. I vaguely remember Gloria getting in bed and putting her arms around me.

I'm not sure of the time, but I heard something hit the wall near the foot of the bed. I flipped on the light on the end table and looked around. To my surprise, I found Gloria stark naked, doing a handstand with her butt against the wall and her firm breasts and stomach facing towards me. I watched as she slowly came down and took a downward dog yoga pose with her butt pointing directly at my face. I was a little confused, but I was impressed with what I saw. Gloria straightened up, grabbed her ankles, and, with her butt still facing me, shook her tight, little bottom at me.

"Interested?"

"Yeah baby," I said, like Austin Powers.

"Let's do it."

Gloria turned, took my hand and raised them above my head. She pulled off my shirt and underwear and teased me with a kiss. She had me like a pot ready to boil over. I leaned over to kiss her when she grabbed my hands and pulled me off the end of the bed.

"Like it rough, huh?" I say, in the best sexy voice I can muster.

"The harder, the better. Now grab your ankles."

"What?"

"Do what I said!"

She took her hands and felt my butt and then, ran them down my legs.

"You have powerful legs. Now, let's put them to work. Ready?"

"Always, baby."

"Good. Now, downward dog," she commanded.

"What?"

"Downward dog."

"What are we doing?" I asked, very confused.

"Yoga, what did you think?"

"I had something else in mind."

"Oh, you men, always thinking about sex," she mumbled, shaking her head.

"Yeah, so?"

"Come on; let's sweat out some of the wine we drank today."

She grabbed my hands and had me contort into positions I never knew I could do or were possible. We were both sweating like crazy when she had me stand back to back with her. She pulled me over her shoulders with her arms interlocked in mine. Both of us are moaning in pain and ecstasy.

"How does this feel?" she grunted.

"Good, I guess," I grunted back.

"How about this?" she said, bending further over.

"Oh my God."

"Ah, you like it."

"Yes."

"How much?"

"I like it a lot," I managed to squeaked out, like Jim Carrey's character in *Dumb and Dumber*.

"Tell me that you love it!"

"I love it!"

"Now, for the finale."

"Thank God," I moaned.

"Handstands."

"You're joking, right? I can't do handstands."

"Sure you can. You do it like this. It's easy."

Gloria turned, flipped onto her hands and landed very lightly against the wall. While she was upside down, her lovely little hoo hoo staring me in the face, she challenged me.

"Come on, you can do it!

"I can't."

"Have faith. See yourself doing it and your mind will make it happen," she assured me.

I took a long, deep breath and leapt on my hands, but was way too far from the wall and I smacked into it violently. My arms gave way and I landed on my head.

"Oh, shit!"

The impact was so hard that it sent pictures on the wall swinging and the lamps on the nightstands wobbled. As I lay on the floor in pain, Gloria somehow found it quite humorous. She placed her hand over her mouth to keep me from seeing that she was laughing her ass off. Soon, tears rolled down her face and she couldn't control her herself.

"Poor baby," she cooed.

However, I was only aware of her ridicule and judgment of my train wreck of a handstand.

The next day, when we were back in the car, Rusty looked at me with a smile on his face, which I could barely see in the rearview mirror, due to my almost broken neck.

"Did you guys feel the earthquake last night?" he asked.

"Earthquake, we didn't feel anything," I stated.

Turning to Gloria, I saw her choking back her desire to laugh at me once more.

Back in Southern California, Gloria and I took a week off from each other. She was a free spirit, much like myself, but she was also very demanding and rigid in many ways. While she wanted a relationship, I was taking time sorting out my feelings for her. One day, while I was at work, she called me.

"Unless you want to put more time into this relationship, we are done," she said.

I told her that I liked her, but that I needed to take things slower and I felt she was demanding too much from me at this time. There was a moment of silence and then, she got upset and told me that it was over. Why not take the plunge and go for it, you might ask. I can only say that when the spirit inside says go, I go. When it's from the head, I have to turn to my heart and ask the question, "What is the thing to do?"

Gloria was a likeable sort, but you just can't force things. That, I would find out very painfully, later in time.

Syrah is the grape that I most associate with Gloria. Dark and almost inky in color, like her skin, the Syrah has lots of dark berry flavors and distinct spiciness. It can grow well in many different soils and climates from Bordeaux France to California to Australia. Sometimes, it is blended with Grenache and other grapes to make a more aromatic, flexible and approachable wine. Being flexible is all about Gloria.

Gabby

I met Gabby after a Blues and Jazz concert in the Valencia Mall. Every summer, they block off the main entrance between the Hyatt and other businesses and feature local Los Angeles bands. It's a free event with wine, beer and local food vendors promoting and selling their products.

I was hanging out with my good friend, Rusty, when I spotted her. She was standing with another woman, but my eyes were drawn to her. She was very interesting to look at. Not only was she attractive, but she had a very unique and interesting profile. She was a thin, light-skinned woman with dark brown eyes and hair. I needed to use the little boy's room, so I headed towards the hotel, where the restrooms were. As I walked by her, I said hello and told her I thought she was pretty. Her eyes lit up and she smiled and thanked me.

When I came back out of the restroom, she and her friend were still standing in the same spot, talking to a couple of other people. I smiled at her as I walked by and she touched my arm.

"I'm Gabby and this is my friend, Robin."

"Oh, hello, I'm Stephen."

"Would you like to join us for the concert?"

"That would be great, but I'm with my friend Rusty."

"Well, he can join us too," Gabby suggested.

Rusty is a very shy man and is married, so no way would he be caught with me and two women that neither of us knew. Santa Clarita is a very "small bedroom" type of community and word spreads like wild fire.

"Thanks for the offer. But, my friend and I need to talk about some things."

"Oh, okay," she said, dejectedly.

I walked away interested, but I did want to hang with Rusty to spend some time catching up on things. The concert ended around 9:30 and Rusty and I walked towards the parking structure. There again, I saw Gabby. She called my name and she and her friend walked over towards us. I introduced Rusty to the both of them and she handed me her card. On the back was her phone number.

"This is my cell number. Give me a call."

"Okay, I will."

"It was great meeting you, Stephen," she added as the two of them turned to walk away. Gabby gave me a smile and one last look.

"Great meeting you, too."

As Rusty and I walked towards our cars, he looked at me and asked, "How do you do that?"

"Do what?"

"Meet women everywhere you go and just like that get their phone numbers?"

He shook his head in wonder.

"I don't know exactly. I just casually compliment them, but then act like I'm not too interested. If you stare or give too much attention, they might think you are needy or a psycho killer," I explained.

"Hmm, well whatever it is, it works for you."

A few days later, I called Gabby and we spoke many times over the next few days. She was easy to talk to and very laid back. We agreed to meet at La Cuisine to have a drink and some appetizers.

I waited almost an hour and a half for her and was ready to leave when she finally showed up. She was frustrated that her son's recital ran way over time and she was a bit edgy. I had just the remedy; I had a bottle of Cabernet already waiting for her. She thanked me and again apologized for being late.

We sat and talked for hours about her two kids, my two kids and all the stuff divorced adults complain and rant about. All in all, she was a good person and a good mother, from what I could gather. We agreed to meet at The Cork in a week to hear my friends' band play. Her kids would be with the ex-husband that weekend, so she had more free time to hang out and have fun.

The weekend arrived and we met at the wine bar. We had an absolute blast talking, drinking, eating and dancing. When it was time to leave, she asked if I had to go home.

"What did you have in mind?" I inquired.

"I don't know, I just don't want to go home."

There is not a lot to do late night in Santa Clarita and so, the options were very limited.

"Well, we could go to my house and try some of my wine and if you're hungry, I cook something up."

"That sounds great," she replied, with a big smile on her face.

She followed me up to my place and, once inside, I started a fire, as it was a little chilly inside the house. I always have trouble keeping my place cool or warm, due to having so many windows. The fact that I am on a hill, where the wind always seems to blow, doesn't help, either. So, I found that a warm fire is always romantic and sets the mood.

I opened a bottle of my Zinfandel and poured it into two of my best glasses. I handed her a glass and I told her I would be right back. I went to the bathroom and changed shirts. When I came back into the living room, I found her sitting completely nude in a chair placed directly in front of the fireplace. I was speechless, but after a moment, I found my voice.

"You okay?"

"Oh, the fire feels so good," she exclaimed as I walked up to her.

"Does it? Are you comfortable?" I asked, as I perused her naked body.

She turned and, with a sexy and confident look, said, "I sure am. Is that a problem?"

It's never a problem when I have a naked woman in my house, but, wow, she feels this relaxed around me? I thought to myself.

I pulled up a chair and sat down next to her.

"You still have your clothes on," she noted.

"Yes, I do."

"Well, something needs to be done about that."

Then, she started undressing me. Even though I knew we were going to have a little fun, I was concerned about the quickness of things. After a few of my other experiences, I was wondering if this is just the way women were these days – fast and furious.

Once I was undressed, we made out and drank wine in the warmth and glow of the fire. Not too long after, we were making love in the bedroom. She stayed the night and then, we went to breakfast the next morning. I was actually starting to feel like Austin Powers, the

International Man of Mystery. I pinched myself and wondered if this was really happening.

We had a good rapport, so I had to ask her why she thought it was okay to take her clothes off in my house when she hardly knew me.

"Weren't you concerned I could do something awful to you?" I asked her.

"Yes, I thought about that, but I just felt so comfortable around you. Something about you and your house just made me feel warm and safe."

"Really, is that so?"

She nodded her head and smiled.

Wow, I said to myself. Have I stumbled upon some magic formula?

Gabby and I dated for a short while, but she was having major issues with her ex. The trials and tribulations of a nasty divorce not only wears on the two ex-spouses, but also everyone else they are involved with.

Also, and this may sound weird, but something about her reminded me of my mother. Mannerisms or the way she spoke or something sent the heebie-jeebies through me when I thought about it. No guy wants to think of his mother when they are being intimate or making love.

We parted company very amicably and, in fact, are great friends. She tells me to this day that her short time with me was the most fun she had ever had with a man. She even told me that she fell in love with me. I only wish that I felt the same way.

Gabby is like Merlot – easy to drink and appreciate. Merlot can be simple or complex with wonderful, soft tannins and dark, berry-like flavors. Easy to grow and appreciate and a versatile wine with food. This was Gabby.

Three Uneventful Dates

By now, I was getting tired of the dating scene, in general, but increasingly so with meeting women on the internet. I was instant messaging a woman on Match.com and I told her that I felt that all of us were like used cars. Some were in better shape than others, with better warranties, and packages, but that we were also carrying years of misuse, unseen damage and overall wear and tear. Of course, many try to hide these imperfections and nicks in our armor with our ego, denial, youth potions and restoration lotions, exercise or cosmetic assistance by plastic surgeons.

Nonetheless, the imperfections and baggage are still there, waiting to be uncovered by our next potential mate. She wrote back, saying that she thought I was being a jerk and that she was no used car sitting on a car lot (internet dating site), waiting for a new owner.

This all brings me to three, somewhat humorous and yet, frustrating internet dates that took place at The Cork. I will present them as if in a montage in a movie, quick and easy.

Shelly

"What made you get a divorce?" I asked Shelley, a slim, white woman with chestnut hair and hazel eyes.

She had no problem telling me and, to this day, I can remember every single word.

"Oh, my husband was a lunatic, lying, no-good son-of-a bitch that screwed every one of my girlfriends and, even my sister. He was a lazy, no-good, philandering bag of horse shit that God mistakenly placed upon this planet to prove that most men are wandering Neanderthals that hunt, fish, fuck and generally cause chaos and discourse in the world and are infinitely stupid and insipid creatures. How about you?"

I took a big sip of wine and just smiled back. What the hell can you say after something like that?

Tilesia

"So, that's why I'm single again," I informed Tilesia, an attractive, curvy, black woman, who I had met on PlentyofFish.com.

She had big, dark eyes and long, hooked fingernails that, if she was provoked, could scratch your eyes out. She just stared at me as she sipped her Chardonnay.

"What about you?" I prodded.

She said nothing, as she gave me the once over.

Okay, I mumbled to myself. I could feel her energy building up, like a tire being filled with too much air.

"Why do you like black women?"

"I like all women."

"Why did you put in your profile that you like women of color?"

"I meant that I like all women, but prefer women who had color to their skin. I simply prefer browner skin to pale white, that's all."

"I don't buy it," she scoffed.

"Buy what?"

"You just think black women are easy and that we will succumb to the power of the white man."

"No, I do not."

"Admit it."

"I can't because it's not true."

"The hell it isn't. You figure if you can take a sister away from a brother, then you have won a victory over the black man."

Then, she did the patented black girl neck roll. I was getting pissed at that point because I have met enough crazy fucking women and this one was about to receive the wrath of all my frustration. So, I let her have it.

"Let me ask you this, girlfriend. Why the hell did you show up to meet me if you think I be bustin' into the brothers' stash and here to take down the black man? Why did you agree to play a part? Huh, you ever thought about that, sister?"

She looked at me with her mouth open in shock, still holding her glass of Chardonnay.

"Well, I –"

"Well, I what? White man got your tongue?"

"You are crazy," she said, as she leaned back in her chair.

"Yes, I am, but not for you, girl. Now, spin around and get your ass out of town," I said loudly enough for some to hear.

As she stormed out, mumbling four-letter words under her breath, Bill gave me the thumbs up. I was jacked up on my ability to no longer take any crazy person's shit.

Patty

Patty was a talkative woman in her early forties with light brown hair and olive skin. To be honest, I didn't want to be there on this date because I already assumed, correctly or not, that this date would be another dud. I was tired of dating, tired of work and overall, just exhausted. I smiled to myself as I thought about Jack Nicholson's line in the movie, *Terms of Endearment*, "I'd rather stick needles in my eyes."

"Do you like to go wine tasting?" I asked, not really caring about her answer.

Like a machine gun she spit out, "Oh, I love to go tasting. I love all kinds of wine – red, white, blush, dry, sweet, fortified, sparkling. I'm really into reds, though."

"What is your favorite?"

"I like wines from California, Chile, Australia, France, South Africa, New Zealand, and Argentina. I love Cabernet, Zin, Barbara, Bordeaux's, Pinot Noir, Cab Franc, Sangiovese, Malbec, and even that silly Merlot that Miles hated in Sideways. Isn't that funny?"

She laughed and made a snorting sound. I put my head in my hands and just stared at her.

"Well, you sure know your wines."

"I know, huh?"

Patty snorts and laughs again.

Time Off –
Meeting Mye

Around January of 2009, I had been on the dating scene for about two years. Burned out from work and women, or rather, the lack of meeting the right one, I became very disenchanted. After talking to my brother, Dino, about a vacation, he and his wife, Joy, told me how much they enjoyed Jamaica and that I should look into it. I found an amazing deal for nine nights and ten days, all-inclusive, in Montego Bay at the Breeze's Hotel on the beach. Believe me, I couldn't wait to get away from my constantly ringing cell phone and problems with customers so that I could get a fresh perspective on women and life, in general. My only intent was to relax on the beach, play some volleyball, explore the island and local culture and to meet and hangout with cool people.

I planned the trip for February 2009 and, at that time, Air Jamaica flew direct to Sangster airport, about six hours each way from LAX. The flight was smooth and hassle-free. When I arrived, I was greeted by a man who first instructed me where to go to catch a van to my hotel and then, tried to sell me vacation excursion packages. I told him I had my itinerary already established, but thanked him for his efforts.

As I waited for my transportation to the hotel, I couldn't help but laugh to myself about a rough-looking gaggle of over weight middle-aged men and women waiting on their bus to the Hedonism resort. Hedonism is well known for nudity, couple-swapping, hooking up with strangers and whatever else might fit your fancy. Much like the Vegas slogan, what happens in Hedonism, stays in Hedonism. Unless, of course, you bring back a little STD with you, that is. I had a very difficult time imagining any of those people walking around naked and shagging each other. I caught my bus to the hotel, which was only about fifteen minutes away. After checking in, I accepted a cold glass of champagne from the doorman who was dressed all in white. As I signed for the room, a drop dead gorgeous, thin, black woman approached me.

"Are you Mr. Wilkins?" she asked.

I noticed she had a rent-a-car shirt on and a pair of keys in her hand. Rarely at a loss for words, I answered her.

"No, but I could be if you wanted me to."

She smiled a big smile and said, in a lovely Jamaican accent, "Mister, you are too funny."

She walked away and my eyes followed her. So did the eyes of the bell hop and doorman. They looked at me, smiled and nodded their heads, as we were all thinking the same thing. Wow!

I arrived at my small, but tidy room on the third floor where I unpacked, then went down to check out the place for a few hours. After that, I returned to the room and fell asleep. I could hear a band playing downstairs, but I was so beat, I just wanted to stay where I was. After all, vacation is about relaxing, not doing so much that you come back more tired than when you left. It was

Saturday night in Jamaica, I was asleep and I was just fine with that.

The next morning, I went down to brunch and had a wonderful Jamaican-style meal. I sat around the large outdoor bar where I met a great deal of people. Mostly snow birds from Canada, Minnesota, Chicago, New York, etc. Over the next week or so, I would bond with some of the people to where years later, we still communicate with each other. It's a rare and special vacation when things like that happen.

After playing volleyball, my bad left knee had swelled to the size of a grapefruit, and I needed a drink. I was more than excited that, just off the beach, they had a self-serve booze and juice bar and I took great advantage of that, trust me. I think I drank more on this trip than in my entire life.

That night, I hung out at the beach bar where they served dinner and had live entertainment. The Jamaican band was quite good and, as part of the show, they lured some poor, wasted guests to come up on stage and do silly things with them. It was a beautiful night in Montego Bay. The moon hung from the heavens as if on a string. There was a warm breeze that made the palm trees sway and chatter. This, coupled with the sound of the ocean waves hitting the sand, was so captivating that I decided to go for walk.

Alone with my thoughts, I was pondering the life I wanted to live in the future. I had always wanted to be able to live wherever I wanted, when I wanted and being a writer would allow me to do just that. As I was designing my new life, I heard someone from behind a palm tree say something.

"Pssst... Hey mon."

I kept walking.

"Hey mon, do you want some weed? Only five dollars," the voice added.

I turned towards the cluster of trees and saw a tall, thin man with missing teeth appear.

"Interested?"

Hell, I'm on vacation. Why not, I thought to myself. So, I decided to buy a couple of joints for five dollars each. I smoked one as I walked the long ribbon of sand before returning the hotel, buzzed from the weed, rum and the feel of the beautiful place.

The next day, I went through much of the same routine – volleyball, swimming, sunning, drinking, eating and conversations with strangers who were fast becoming friends. That night, the band was back, but they put on a variety type show. I sat at the oval-shaped bar and was served by Tikka, a sweet, black woman with large eyes and a great sense of humor. I asked her what drink she liked to make and when she said how about a "Naked on the Beach", I laughed and did my impression of Austin Powers, "Oh behave, baby." As I sipped my drink and listened to the band, I glimpsed across the bar and saw a woman with the most intriguing set of eyes. They reminded me of the eyes most movies portray Cleopatra as having. Piercing and alluring, with upturned corners and pupils as black as coal. I asked Tikka who she was.

"Oh, baby, that's Mye. Do you want to meet her?"

"No, she's with someone."

"Nah, dat's the guy who works here. Let me introduce you."

"No, I will do it," I informed her.

I waited until the man left and I walked around the bar to sit next to her.

"May I sit here?"

"Yes," she said.

She had this look that is hard to describe – very ethnic, charismatic and classy. Her jet-black skin brought out her luscious eyes even better.

"I'm Stephen," I said, I turning to shake her hand.

"I'm Mye."

I looked at those eyes and couldn't help but say, "My, oh my, you have beautiful eyes."

She laughed and blushed.

"Oh, tank you, dat's sweet."

We sat and talked about things for about twenty minutes or so when she suddenly said that she had to go.

"Where?" I asked.

"Baby, I'm de singer in de band. Maybe we can talk later."

I watched her walk with a sexy sway away from me and to the side of the stage. Moments later, the MC handed her the microphone and the band broke into an energetic, Jamaican tune. With microphone in hand, Mye started dancing and shaking her body like I had never seen before. She worked the stage with an energetic, passionate fervor. Her voice was slightly raspy, yet controlled and powerful. I watched as she shook her hips wildly and sang her heart out.

We never got to talk after the show because the band had to leave and they were her ride home. She waved goodbye as they all walked out together.

It wasn't the last time I would see her though, as the next day and every day after that, we would have dinner at the resort together. After every long day of drinking, sightseeing and hanging out at the beach, I would get the wonderful opportunity to have dinner with Mye.

The staff gave me crap every day that I was "The Chosen One." When I asked what that meant, they would say, "Mye never talks or has dinner whit anyone. You are de first. You are de Chosen One." Well, I felt good about knowing that our interlude was not a customary thing with her and maybe, I was something special to her.

We never got too personal and, in reality, nothing was going to happen except a little flirting. If she was caught in my room, she would be fired and she could not afford that. Life in Jamaica is hard. Everyone works to simply exist and yet, they love the same toys, phones, and clothes as we do. Mye was also a woman of character and integrity. I would not do anything to hurt her or jeopardize her job.

One night, I took part in the talent show for guests of the hotel. The host for the show, Sean, and I had become buddies and he asked me if I would dance.

"Sean, have you seen me dance?"

"Yes, de night you were drunk and were doing de Austin Powers dance."

"So, there you go. I'm sure it wasn't pretty."

"I loved it. You were funny, mon."

"Sean, I won't dance, but can I play piano and sing 'Great Balls of Fire'?"

"Sure ting," Sean replied.

Mye was present that night when my name was called and I approached the stage. She seemed surprised I was going to do something. The keyboard player reluctantly surrendered his instrument to me and Sean had to hold the microphone since there was no proper stand. I told the band what I was going play and they seemed unfamiliar with the song, so I played solo.

The song's beginning is unmistakable and, from the start, all the people started dancing and singing to, "You shook my nerves and you rattled my brain/ too much loving drives a man insane/ You broke my will, oh what a thrill/ Goodness gracious, Great balls of fire!" Soon, the band got the feel of the song and jumped in. When the song ended, the place exploded with applause. As I left the stage, a normally calm and somewhat restrained Mye grabbed me.

"You didn't tell me you could play and sing," she said, darting her eyes side to side, as if too shy to look me in the face. "You were damn good, mon."

I felt honored that she thought I was good. After all, this woman was really, really talented. She had an amazing voice, was pretty, had great poise and was a killer dancer.

The next night, Mye had most of the night off, so she hung out with me at Breezes. We went upstairs and I played piano for her and a couple of drunks that asked me to play silly country songs.

After everyone left, the TV, which was an old, outdated rear projection big screen, was playing the movie *300*. Mye sat in one of the two leather chairs and watched the movie. I sat down next to her. There was no sound and, being the goof ball I am, I started making up stupid lines they would say to each other instead of the actual dialogue. Mye was laughing and crying at my antics.

Moments later, the guitarist from the band came up to tell her they were packing up and would be going soon. We looked at each other and she got a little misty-eyed. My heart sunk from my chest as I knew this might be the last time I would see her.

We walked downstairs and outside where the musicians were packing up and some of my newfound friends were standing around, talking to them. Mye turned to me and asked, "What time are you leaving tomorrow?"

I told her I was unsure that being on vacation made me lose track of things. I never will forget that look she gave me. Her eyes started to tear and she handed me a little piece of paper folded together. She quickly turned and walked away towards the front of the hotel.

"Open it," Alicia suggested.

I unfolded the little piece of paper to read what she had written and I was greatly touched.

"Read it out loud," Bobbie demanded.

> *From the moment I saw your beautiful, green eyes staring at me from across the bar, I knew you were my soul mate. I love you.*
> *Signed,*
> *Mye*

Below the note were two phone numbers.

"Oh my God, go after her. She might be the one," Alicia told me.

I took one more look at the letter and did as she suggested. She was in the lobby, waiting for the guys to pull the van around. I ran to her, held her in my arms and kissed her forehead and cheek, knowing that if I went too far, the bellhop or cameras might see us and get her fired. She had tears in her eyes as she looked up at me.

The horn sounded as the musicians watched us from the van that was parked at the front of the hotel. She gave me a kiss on the cheek and was gone. I slowly walked back to my friends as if I was facing the inquisition. Everyone asked me questions, rapid-fire.

"What happened?"

"Are you going to see her?"

"Do you love her?"

Then, Alicia looked me straight in the eye and said, "My God, you could have so much fun together. With her singing and dancing and your musical ability, you guys could be amazing."

I was thinking the same thing and was quite excited by the thought.

On the final day in a place that I enjoyed so much, I was uneasy, almost sad, about heading home. I surely had no desire to return to my job at Super Foods, where the minute I got back, I would have a million problems and issues to deal with. Actually, I dreaded the thought.

As I counted down the last few moments of my time in this wonderland, I sat and talked to Alicia and Keith. We had a few drinks before I was notified that the dreaded shuttle to the airport had arrived. They asked me if I had heard from Mye. I told them I had left messages on her phone, but she didn't answer. I felt in my soul that she would show up at the hotel at the very last minute to say a passionate goodbye, like in some Hollywood movie. Sadly, that never happened.

As I reluctantly boarded the shuttle, my heart felt completely empty and lost. I wanted to get to know this intriguing creature of a woman and yet, this was goodbye. The fifteen-minute ride to the airport seemed like forever and once there, I kept looking for her in the crowd. I had to ask myself why I expected her to be there. This wasn't some Hollywood romance movie; this was real life. Things like that just don't happen. Then, I sold myself on the idea that it was just a fling, a temporary moment of being enamored with someone. Let it go.

I went through customs and was waiting to board the plane when my cell phone rang.

"Stefan, where are you?"

"Mye?"

"Yes, baby, where are you?"

"I'm boarding the plane, where are you?"

"Stefan, I am in the airport and I have been looking for you for almost an hour. I want to see you," she said, frantically.

I was breathless for a second.

"Mye, honey, I have to get on the plane. I will call you when I get home to LA."

"Stefan, I miss you already," she said, with a quiver in her voice.

"I miss you, too."

An announcement was made for final boarding of my flight.

"Mye, I have to go. I will call you later," I said, as I headed to the plane.

"Bye, Stefan," she sobbed.

There is nothing more enticing than Mye's voice. It is innocent, yet sultry and, coupled with her accent, downright sexy. She pronounced my name like no other woman has and that will live with me all of my life.

Every moment of the flight home, I was thinking of her. As soon as I landed, I took out my dying cell phone and found four missed calls and three text messages from her. I wasn't able to respond until I got home around 12:30 in the morning. The moment I plugged my phone into the charger, it rang.

"Hello, this is Stephen."

"Baby, you scared me. I was waiting to hear if you got home safe," Mye's voice rang out.

"Baby Mye, I am fine."

There was a long pause and I could hear her breathing and choking on her tears. I was so enamored with this woman that we talked until three a.m., my time and six a.m., hers. I loved to hear the musical sound of her voice. I could feel her through the phone, as if we were cosmically connected. I so badly wanted to wrap my arms around her and kiss those beautiful eyes and lips.

For days, I was useless, as my mind was on her. Was Mye real or an illusion, I asked myself. I was possessed and had to hear her voice and talk to her every day. My first cell phone bill was $700. I was so crazy about her that I never even thought about the charges. I wised up, however, and bought a discount card from Penny Talk and we could chat for days.

She let me know her birthday was coming up in March and I immediately made plans to go see her. And that's when I realized that the topic of age had never come up for either of us and, as they say in Jamaica, age is just a number.

I knew from dating women of color that it is hard to know how young or old they are. They don't seem to show their age like woman of lighter skin color do. I remember when I was dating Gloria that when she said she told me how old she was, I was very surprised. That's when Gloria told me the secret: "black don't crack." I never knew anything could even happen between Mye and me, so why should I care about how old or young she was? All I knew she was that she was a hell of a woman.

I tried to book my flight to see her and was told that Air Jamaica was out of business. They were bankrupt. So, there were no more direct flights. I chose the best flight

I could, but all the choices had long layovers and multiple connections. That's the price you pay for booking at short notice.

I ultimately chose American Airlines that flew to Dallas/Fort Worth, then to Miami and then to Jamaica. It seemed like days but I finally arrived. Mye told me she would be there to pick me up and to look for her.

After getting through customs, where they tore through everything in my bag, I walked out of the airport looking for a shorthaired Mye, which was the hairstyle she had had when I last saw her. As I walked out among the hundreds waiting for friends, taxies or buses, I spied the backside of a woman in jeans with long hair and a walk that would knock any man's eyes out of their sockets. She went into the ladies room outside the airport building. A Jamaican man was standing next to me handling bags and he saw me looking at her.

"Hot, isn't she?" he announced.

I nodded and continued to look for Mye. When I had almost given up, someone touched me on the shoulder and asked, "Stefan?"

It was Mye and she was the woman with long hair that I had watched walk into the bathroom. She gave me the biggest hug and I couldn't have been more excited and happy to see her again.

At a bar outside the airport arrival area, we sat and had a beer while waiting on her taxi. We just stared at each other. I could feel her and words were not necessary. Soon, the driver arrived and we left in his car to her house. I would be staying four days with Mye and whatever accommodations she had.

The ride from the airport to her home passed all the high-end resorts, flashy clubs and restaurants and went into an area of small homes and apartments. Weaving his way up a hill and around a few sharp corners, the driver pulled up to a house with an old man sitting on the porch. Mye and I walked past him and to her little house sitting on the same property. I could feel him watching us, so I turned to look at him. He smiled at me with half his teeth gone and nodded. I nodded back. As she unlocked the door, I asked who he was.

"Mr. Cook. He bothers me 'cause he is watching me all de time," she said.

"Well, even old men still love beautiful, young women."

Her place was small, but well kept. I entered straight into the bedroom that also served as a living room. There was a small bathroom and a tiny kitchen. She pointed out that there was no hot water, but who needs it in Jamaica, anyway?

I put my bag on the couch and opened it up. I searched through the bag and found a silver, lame scarf I had bought for her.

"Happy Birthday!" I announced.

She grabbed it, smelled it and put it around her neck. She walked over to the little mirror in the bathroom and exclaimed, "I love it, Stefan."

She took another look before giving me a kiss and a huge hug.

"Do you know how much I have missed you?" she whispers in my ear.

"Do you know how much I have missed you?" I asked.

I reached into my bag and pulled out three bottles of my wine that I brought to share with her. She read the label and, again, the way she said my name sent chill bumps up my spine.

"Stephen Hemmert Vineyards," she read, pronouncing it as, Stefan Hammer Vanyars. "I bet its good, jest like you."

She took the night off from work to be with me, which had cost her quite a deal of money, so I told her that I would take her out to dinner. We both showered and got ready to go when she requested that we just head into town to get fish from a street vendor.

"It's de best fish in town. Let me call de driver," she announced.

In Jamaica, if you don't have a car, you try to hook up with someone who is a reliable, somewhat dedicated taxi driver. In a way, they almost become a chauffeur.

"Why don't we walk?" I asked.

"Baby, it's a couple of miles into town and its nighttime. Dat's not an option." she made clear.

As she continued to get dressed, I played around with an old guitar she had.

"Can you play dat?" she asked.

"A little."

I tuned it the best I could and played one of my own songs called, "Only Heaven Knows."

"Who did dat song? It's lovely," she inquired.

"It's mine," I told her.

"Wow, dat's beautiful, Stefan."

I could tell she was impressed, as she gave me "that look." Something in that look told me I was really important to her. I was hoping that I was.

I had brought her some CD's of artists I liked, such as Crowded House, Amos Lee, Corinne Bailey Rae and others, as well as some DVD's, including *Austin Powers*, *Dumb and Dumber*, *The Notebook*. Later, we would lie in each other's arms as we watched these movies on my computer, as she had no TV or video player. These are some of my favorite memories and they were nothing, but two people sharing a heartbeat and a breath, living for the moment.

So, that night, we went to the town for fish. I told her I would buy, but she insisted she would pay. She told me that I had to order the fish and pay with Jamaican dollars, not US. She told me that she wanted to see how well I could handle myself with her people.

The street was filled with music, cars and people. Some were walking the narrow sidewalks, some were shopping and others just hung out, talking. There were people leaning against buildings and walls, others perched on railings and steps to the humble apartments that lined the street. Somehow this scene reminded me of my childhood in Oklahoma way before cable, DVD's, CD's and cell phones. People would grab a beer or iced tea and sit out in their lawns or porches and just be. That really doesn't exist much anymore and so, this reminded me of earlier times in my life and in the world.

We arrived at the corner where the fish guy was. They had two grills going and were steaming fish in foil with collard greens, okra, garlic and other spices. This also took me back home to Oklahoma, where my mom used to cook lots of okra and collard greens. The memories came wafting back to me like a soft summer breeze. I asked the fish man what he had.

"Me got fish either four ounce or six," he shouted, with little patience.

"Give me two six ounce!" I shouted over the crowd.

"Comin up, man."

I was the lone white person and I know I stood out like a sore thumb. After all, the area we were in was not one normally visited by the typical tourist crowd. I felt no fear or judgment from anyone. I was awash in the scenery of the local people walking, talking, playing music, laughing and flirting with each other.

I could see Mye's eyes peering at me from inside the car and I wondered how I was doing. He packed up the fish and asked me for 400 dollars. At first, I flinched, but remembered it was around 86 Jamaican to the US dollar. I went through the various bills and gave him 420 Jamaican and told him keep the change. Maybe not much of a tip, but at least I gave him something. I grabbed the paper bags and headed back to the car.

Once inside, she looked at me, counted the money and announced, "You did well, my man. Some Jamaican people try to mess whit de tourists, but you did good."

The driver took us back to her place and we listened to the Crowded House CD I had brought her while we ate the fish and drank some of my wine. It was hot in the house, so we sat outside on her little porch. She sat glued to my left side and as we talked, I fed her every bite. Again, there is something so romantic about this simple act of feeding and caring for someone. I felt the heat between us and the energy of two passionate souls and yet, there was such calm, feeling of comfort.

We only could eat one of the fish, so we saved the other for later. Soon, we were all talked out, tired and ready for bed. I asked her if we should sleep together.

"Unless you don't like me?" she asked.

That was definitely not the case, so we climbed into bed together. Crowded House was still playing on her computer when I heard her scream.

"Owe!"

"What happened?" I asked, with concern.

"Did you hear what da man said in de song?"

"No, I didn't."

"Play it again," she said, almost jumping out of her skin.

I did and I heard what she was talking about. It's one of my favorite Crowded House songs, "Fall at your Feet." The opening line is, "I'm really close tonight." She screamed again.

"Did you hear it, Stefan, he sang, 'I'm really close to Mye.'"

She dipped her chin down and stared at me with those eyes and gave me a kiss. I didn't care that she had misinterpreted the word "tonight" for "Mye." Whatever made her happy would eventually make me happy, as well.

I promised myself I would be good and not come onto to her sexually. Regardless of the passion I may feel, I would abstain, as I wanted to get to know her more. But then, hours later, when I was asleep, little Elvis popped up to say hello.

It was how her skin felt against my body; it was, like chocolate satin. I kissed the back of her neck and she responded. I continued down her neck to her back and she took a deep breath and sighed. We were already naked, as the nights and days in Jamaica were hot and steamy and now, they were getting even hotter. She rolled over towards me and we kissed. Her lips were full and inviting. I kissed her eyes and forehead and then made my way down to her neck, to her shoulders and ultimately arriving on her breasts with large, succulent, protruding nipples.

From there we spent what seemed to be hours just exploring and discovering each other. Mye was soft and yet, muscular. She was confident and yet, vulnerable and I treated her as such. Later, we fell asleep, only to wake the next morning still in each other's arms.

Over the next few days and nights, we hung out, enjoying each other's company. One day, we ventured off to the store where I could buy food to prepare for her. I love to cook and she loved to eat, so it was perfect combination. I must admit that it was challenging to cook what I wanted on her little one flame, propane-driven cook top. She also possessed only a small, dorm room-style refrigerator that would hold a few precious items. I made her pasta, steak, garlic mashed potatoes and other things that pleased her fancy.

On another day, I followed her through town, looking for the right place to get her nose pierced. I told her I wanted to buy her something more for her birthday and this was something she desired. It was comical as I was the only white person in this part of Montego Bay. Not a tourist or wanderer in sight. I felt confident and unafraid, but there were times when guys tried to harass me for money and a few snarled and barked their disapproval when they saw me hold hands with Mye. I figured they were just jealous because I was with one of "their" beautiful women.

We stumbled upon a cute shop where I bought her an orange summer dress. When she tried it on and showed it to me, I almost fainted. It fit her perfectly.

The third day I was there was her actual birthday and I wanted to do something special for her. I remembered that on my last trip, I had been to a place called the Luminescent Lagoon. It is an amazing place where at night, anything that moved lit up because of the living phosphorus in the water. They get stirred up by the boat, propeller, fish and even you, should you decide to get in and wave around a bit. I made reservations and we called her driver to take us there.

First, I made her dinner, we had some of my wine and made love before the driver arrived. The lagoon was about an hour or more outside of Montego Bay. We had to pass through the little town of Falmouth, where people lined the streets talking, playing music, dancing and just hanging out. Kids approached the taxi asking for money, which is one of the drawbacks of this beautiful place. Outside the hotels, you're besieged by locals asking for money or looking to take you to some exotic spot for a fee. I have heard that sometimes, they take you someplace special, only to rob you and leave you without a dime to find a way back to your hotel.

Once we got to our destination, we boarded the old, wooden boat and set out on the water. Mye held me the whole time, squeezing me like we were going to die. I looked at her and realized that she was crying.

"Mye, what's wrong?"

"Nobody's ever done something like dis for me. Dis is the happiest day of my life."

For me, there are moments in a day, a month, a year or a lifetime you remember that really make you feel good and this was one of those moments.

She watched with awe as fish illuminated the water as they swam around us. A few, brave souls jumped in to wave their arms and pretend for a brief moment that they were angels with blue, luminescent wings. Neither Mye, nor I had any intention of jumping into the dark, cool water. After all, I would have had to pry her off me in order to toss her in; she hung onto me like an octopus.

"Look at de sky, Stefan," she said, as she pointed to the heavens. "I've never seen so many stars, as if they are here for just me and you to see."

She kissed me and tucked her head under my arm and onto my chest.

Back at the dock, we summoned the driver and headed home to her place. In the car, she never let go of me, even for a moment. I can only describe her this night as an innocent, little girl, who had to grow up way too fast in order to find her place in this world. Mye had been on her own since the age of fifteen when her parents split up. Her dad lived in Kingston, which was over three hours away, and her mother remarried and lived somewhere in New York.

At her home, we laid in each other's arms, not really talking, just listening to music and each other's heartbeat.

"Mye, not that it's important, but how old are you?" I suddenly asked.

"You're right, it's not important."

"Mye, I don't care because I know who you are, but I still would like to know."

She paused for a moment before answering.

"23."

I lost my breath and coughed.

"What?"

"See I told you that it wasn't important and now, you made it so. I knew dat would be your reaction."

"Mye, why didn't you tell me before?" I asked.

"Because I loved you from the moment our eyes met. I sat at da bar and when I saw dos green eyes connect wit mine, I knew!" she exclaimed.

"Okay, so you knew, but why not tell me before?"

"Because you would not have come back and dat's because you Americans are so hung up on shit like age. Age is just a number and me fata was twenty plus years older dan me mata and nobody cares, but you Americans judge everyting, not by love or feelings, but by money, looks and age."

She had a point. We, in the US, judge things much differently than other parts of the world. Truth was, I really didn't care about her age, but in the US, I would be chastised for even thinking about dating or being in love with a woman her age. But I was in Jamaica and I was with a woman I fell for in a very short time. I wanted to spend as much time as I could with her, to hell with age, to hell with everything. If I died tonight, I would be the happiest man in the world.

I only had one more day and night in Jamaica with Mye. Again, I was depressed at the thought of having to come back to LA and to my job at Super Foods and an empty home. Although Jamaica was dog-eat-dog as well, the people seemed more content with just living. My life at home was that of mortgages, car payments, college tuition and ever-mounting taxes and bills. If I didn't sell, I didn't get paid. So, I had to push and fight to make money in order to keep my lifestyle and my kids in school. I thought about the simple way in which Mye lived and how it had its advantages.

Mye was performing at Breezes that night and I got to see Tikka, Sean and some of the crew I had met just a month earlier. I was a guest of the hotel, so drinks and food were on the house. Mye got up to the microphone and before launching into her first song, pointed to me and said, "Dis song is for my man out there, Mr. Stefan Hammer."

I was in awe as she blasted out the song, "I Will Always Love You" by Whitney Houston. After the song, a couple from New York came up to me. They both smiled.

"You are a very lucky man," the woman said.

I thought that I was too.

After the show, Mye seemed a little down. It was raining buckets and the night air had a slight chill to it as we went back to her place. She said she wanted to take a shower and just lie with me. I suggested she take a long, hot bath, but then remembered she had no hot water, which meant no bath. Call me a hopeless, helpless romantic, but I decided to make her a one anyway.

As she lay on the bed watching me with a big smile on her face, I took plastic and covered up the drain hole in her shower. There was six-inch lip around the shower stall that would at least hold some water, so I began the tedious job of heating pots of water one after another to fill the shower basin. Finally, after thirty to forty-five minutes, the basin was full. I took Mye's hand and introduced her to her royal, makeshift bath. She eased into it and once in, looked at me and said, "Stefan, I love you."

"I love you, too, Mye." I said back, without hesitation.

Something about caring for Mye was so ingrained in me and made me feel so good in the process, that I never doubted the 'L' word. I just enjoyed being with and around her. Hearing her speak and laugh, watching her sing and dance. For the first time since Mary, I felt like I was falling in love.

The next morning, we were up, sharing some breakfast and talking. She put on the orange dress I bought her and kept saying how much she was going to miss me. The driver arrived to take us to the airport and when we were halfway there, we stopped at a place where we could see a beautiful view of the ocean. We went to a little restaurant and dress shop that overlooked the ocean on a steep cliff, which she said was her favorite place. We had pictures taken of us there, one of which still melts my heart when I see it. We held each other, looking out over the shimmering, blue water and not a word was spoken. We knew this was it, at least for now, but maybe forever.

Arriving at the airport, I retrieved my luggage from the trunk of the car and said goodbye to the man who had been our driver and chauffeur. Mye grabbed my hand and together, we went to check the luggage and get my boarding pass. As we waited in line, Mye held onto my hand so tight that I started to lose feeling in it. Her palms, which were always moist, were now dripping with sweat. She wrapped her arms around me tightly and buried her head in my chest. She looked up at me with those big, Egyptian-looking eyes and started weeping.

When my bag was checked in and it was time to go, I wrapped my arms around her. I placed a kiss on her forehead and began to cry myself. There we were, two people from different parts of the world, two people of different cultures and race, years apart in age, in the middle of Sangster Airport, crying about leaving each other.

She slowly pulled away and walked out the front of the airport and to the glass window. She stood in a mass of tears and waved goodbye once more before getting back into the car. I walked towards customs, trying to hide the flow of tears that ran down my face. I would eventually board the plane without Mye and without my heart.

It could have ended there and simply been a beautiful, romantic, love won/love lost movie script, but it didn't. Now, more than ever, I wanted her and she wanted me. I bought her a laptop so we could communicate with each other. She would send me pictures and videos of her shows and of people I knew, telling me to come back to Jamaica.

The Best of Intentions / Twist of Fate

Mye was very spiritual and self-sufficient woman. Even though life was tough there, she was always motivated to better herself and the life of her two-year-old son, who I didn't meet and, from what I understood, spent most of the time under the care of his grandmother. Yes, I know. What fifty-four-year-old guy would want a twenty-three-year-old woman with a two-year-old son? Call me stupid, but she rocked my world and there wasn't anything spiritually, physically or otherwise that I wouldn't do for her.

We decided she would come for a visit to the US in June. I want to tell you now: I feel our government is racist when it comes to certain countries that it feels is undesirable and Jamaica is one of those countries. I consulted with friends and associates of mine who had married aliens or had visitors from foreign countries come over to visit them. I also researched all I could on the website, "Visa-Journey" to make sure everything we did was legal.

Mye and I planned to get her a simple ten-day visitor's passport or permit to the US. She had money in the bank, a letter from her employers, the store she worked in and the hotel. She had a letter from her ex-husband that he and his mother were watching her child and even an itinerary of where she was going in the US, and why.

To file, she had to drive all the way to Kingston, which is over three hours from Montego Bay. So, the trip would not be wasted, we went over everything repeatedly as she was quite nervous. We could not have one slip up, as the US Immigration would notice the slightest faux pas.

She left Montego Bay at four a.m. to make it to the US Embassy in Kingston by eight. Once there, she had to wait in a long line that stretched outside the building and into the lawn to be interviewed. I meditated and asked God that if we are to be together, to please bring her to me so we could see each other again. If not, let me know why and show me a sign.

I wished I could be there for her during that stressful time. However, in the months since coming back from visiting her on her birthday, I suffered a huge drop in income, due to the recession. I lost ten profitable accounts in a very short period and, with two kids in college, I was hurting financially. I bring this up because I had sent what money I had to her to purchase a ticket, transportation and the like. I was not in a financial position to fly to Jamaica to see her, although I would be there now if I could.

Since Jamaica is three hours ahead of me here in California, I got her call at around nine a.m., my time. She was crying and very upset.

"Mye, what happened?" I asked.

"Stefan, everyting was going fine. She ask me about why I want to go to America, where I was going, who I would see, who was taking care of my son. Everyting that we went over."

"And?"

"Everyting was good and den, she ask about my mata."

"The one that lives in New York?"

"Yes, and I tell de lady, I've not seen her since I was six, but I have her address and everyting."

"Okay, nothing wrong there."

"Yes, but den she ask me about someone I don't know and I say, should I know this person? The lady take my application and stamps, denied."

"Shit, did you know this person they asked you about?"

"No, Stefan, I have no idea who she is," she answered, choking on her tears.

"Never heard her name before?"

"Never."

"OK, Mye, we will work on it and try again next month."

"No, I can't reapply for nine months."

Why, on the basis of that one question, would they deny her a ten-day visitor's visa? I was angry beyond words as Mye and I finished our conversation. Then, as per my prayers or some unknown lack of belief in Mye and me getting together, God or fate stepped in.

Before we examine fate, I want to take a second to explain what happened when I was so distraught about Mye not being able to visit, I contacted a psychic to ask a simple question.

"I met someone; please tell me about her."

His reading freaked me out.

"You are from two different cultures and countries. She is black and you are white. This woman loves you very much and is much younger than you," the psychic said.

"Why is she not able to come to me if all this was true?" I asked.

"The timing is not quite right at this moment, but know this: this woman is your true soul mate. You are of the same spirit and you must be together. Please hear me: you must not let go of this woman. She is your other half."

I was speechless. I mentioned to the psychic about the difference in our ages and how I was okay with it, but others wouldn't be.

"If you are worried about what others think, then you have imprisoned yourself from your true nature and desires. Do your friends or relatives pay your mortgage, car payment or bills?" he asked.

"No."

"Then, why do you let the opinions of others deter you from being with the woman you love and should be with? Let me pose this to you: if you had ten amazing years together, would this not be better than having nothing together? Do not let this woman go!"

Mye (pun intended) grape for her is my beloved Zinfandel, also known as Primitivo in Italy. Mye was soft and approachable yet, possessed perfect structure. Wonderful dark berry fruit balances in a fine Zinfandel. Zinfandel is thin-skinned and ripens unevenly and there is nothing you can do to change it. It rarely provides a super dark wine or tannic harshness and leans toward being fruity, spicy and overall, a very honest, enjoyable wine. That indeed is and was Mye.

Luna (Part One)

Back in January of 2009, before meeting Mye, I was working on an account that I really wanted. They were a very successful restaurant and getting the owners to give me a shot at their business was not an easy thing to do. One day, I was schmoozing with the female owner and I remarked about a beautiful, exotic woman by the name of Luna who waited on me at the restaurant.

"Oh, she's going to be here in a few moments," the owner said. "Do you want to meet her?"

"Is she single?" I asked.

"Yes, she is. I'll introduce you."

They were closing up and I didn't want to be in their way, so I went outside. While on my cell phone, I noticed Luna had arrived, and was in the back of the restaurant, unloading groceries. She was hard to miss – caramel skin, jet-black hair and eyes to match. She looked Asian, along with an intoxicating mixture of other things. I felt no harm in entering through the back door to see if she needed help unloading her van. Once inside, I saw her at a table in the kitchen. I slowly walked up to her and introduced myself.

"Hi, I'm Stephen."

She looked at me like I was from Mars, but I continued.

"You waited on me the other day."

"What are you doing in my kitchen?" she asked with an intense frown.

I looked around, wondering if the kitchen of the restaurant had suddenly become hers. Nope, still the restaurant's kitchen.

"Well, I told the owner I wanted to meet you and say hello."

As I smiled at her, she glared at me.

"I thought maybe you could join me for a glass of wine tonight," I continued.

"My kids and I bake together on Friday nights."

"Oh, you have kids. How many?"

"Three," she shot back, with a "you're wasting my time" look.

"Oh."

I don't want to date anyone with kids, I thought to myself. My two were grown and in college. I could feel she was uncomfortable about me being in her presence and I could feel a lot of negative energy.

"Anyway, I'm dating somebody," she said.

Now, here's the deal: this woman had the most amazing face I have ever seen, not to mention unbelievably perfect skin. I know she probably gets hit on more than a batting practice baseball, so I get her being elusive and strong, but come on.

"Interesting, I was told you were single."

"By whom?"

"The owner."

"She would not have said that; she's knows I with somebody," Luna said, sharply.

Just then, the owner stuck her head around the corner.

"Luna, Stephen wants to meet you. Oh, I see that's already happened."

She disappeared as quickly as she appeared, somewhat embarrassed, I think.

"Well, I'm not single. I'm dating somebody," she insisted.

"Okay, well, you can't blame a guy for trying, can you?"

"I don't know, can you?" she spat back with venom.

Again, I love a gal with a little piss and vinegar, as my mom would say, but, to be honest, she was mean and had no problem being that way. This was going nowhere and, after all, if she was this nasty early on, what would she be like once I were with her a while? My intuition and experience told me to leave this one alone.

This crush of my ego, along with other things I had been through with women and work, were the catalyst to go to Jamaica. There, of course, I met Mye. Now here's where it gets weird, so follow me.

I believe if you really want something bad enough, you pray, focus your energy and work towards getting it and, if everything is in alignment, it eventually it will happen.

I truly wanted to be with Mye, but, if you remember, I asked God if we were meant to be to make it happen. I didn't want to push fate, nor could I. We had planned, prayed and worked on it for months. I asked God that if she can't come and if I'm meant to be with someone else, to please point me in the right direction or give me a sign. So, this very same day that I got the news about Mye not being able to come to see me, God gave me a message, alright, albeit one I did not expect.

I was depressed about Mye and had no interest in going into work. I had no desire to mask my emotions by putting on a face and pretending to be happy. I walked into the restaurant where Luna worked, whose business I had finally earned, and started to do the order. I could see her watching me. She approached and asked if I wanted anything. I ordered a country fried steak and eggs and a passion fruit iced tea. She put the order in and quickly returned.

"Can I ask you something? What sign are you?"

"Scorpio," I said.

"Oh, shit." she muttered and, without an explanation, she walked away.

What the hell does that mean, I thought to myself.

Later, she reappeared and I asked her, "Okay, so you asked me my sign, what's yours?"

She just smiled seductively and walked away. That's when she got me interested and she knew how to play me. I approached her at the bar where she was making drinks.

"That's kind of unfair. I told you when you asked me."

She smiled with her beautiful smile and looked me in the eye.

"What do you think I am?"

"Scorpio," I said, with confidence.

"Yep, you got it."

"See, it takes one to know one."

I went back in my seat and I could feel her looking at me. I tried to act cool, but I was still very attracted to her, even though I had been very rudely turned down the first time I met her. I watched her as she sailed about the restaurant. She was sexy and sensual, and she knew it. So, this woman who dissed me in January was now flirting with me in June, the very same day I found out Mye couldn't be with me. She brought over the check and looked at me.

"Well, I hope to see you again, Scorpio."

Then, she turned and walked away. I watched her leave and reveled in how this woman could be so hot and know just how to play it. She had got to be trouble. Still reeling from Mye, I had no desire to pursue her, though.

Days later, I was invited to the restaurant by my friend, Asa. Our conversation turned to a wine festival that we wanted to attend called "Wine in the Pines." Luna was our server and she overheard our conversation. Once Asa left, I stayed to do the order and she approached me.

"I heard you say that you are going to the wine festival in Pine Mountain?"

"Yes, we are," I replied.

"I'd like to go."

"Well, you and your boyfriend can get tickets by going on the website. I think its forty dollars."

"We're not together anymore and I'd like to go with you."

"Well, okay, you can ride with Asa and me. We can pick you up at 10:00."

Here's where the charm of a beautiful woman begins.

"I only want to be with you," she pouted.

Now, right here, if I had followed my instincts, I could have avoided so much pain and anguish later on. But guess what, I didn't, so shame on me.

"Wow, well, Asa and I already agreed to go and meet some friends there," I replied.

"Please?" she asked, batting her eyes and pouting.

"Let me think about it," I said, with no intention of ditching my friend for a hot woman.

When I talked to Asa, he, being a friend and gentleman, told me to use his ticket for her and for us to go and have fun. I thanked him for understanding and the next day, I told her we were on.

The weird thing was that she never made the trip with me. Asa and I were at the restaurant the day before the wine tasting and Luna was having breakfast with one of her daughters. Even though we sat right next to them, she acted somewhat cold and reserved. An hour or so later, I called to let her know when I was picking her up on Saturday. I got her voicemail and, hours later, she called back to tell me that she couldn't go. Her ex couldn't pick up the kids. I was a little frustrated and I let her know that for her to wait until the last minute put me in a bad spot.

"Sorry, I can't help it that my ex is an asshole," she said, tersely.

So, Asa was back on to go with me. During the event, we talked about how I should avoid Luna, by virtue of the way she had originally treated me, as well as her selfish request to only be with me, knowing I would have to change plans with my friends.

"She is selfish and a flake. Let her go," Asa said.

The fact that Luna did not come to the event with me was bad enough, but to double the insult, my former girlfriend, Mary, was there, looking better than ever. She was living a few minutes away from Pine Mountain and was there with her brothers. I had to endure seeing the former love of my life, looking hot and asking me why I had no date. I claimed Asa as my date.

"Sorry," Asa said. "You're not quite my type."

The next week, I was in the restaurant and Luna apologized for not being able to make the event. I was calm and cool and told her that she missed out. Again, something told me to let this one slide. But, she was charming, knew exactly what she was doing and, with little effort, got me into inviting her to go out for a glass of wine.

I picked her up at her apartment and she was waiting outside for me. She was mesmerizing in a gold and copper dress that accented her jet-black hair and glowing, caramel skin. She was quite breathtaking. We went to The Cork on our first real date to see The Acoustics play. A woman sitting in front of us kept turning to look at us, which made me a little uncomfortable. She finally looked at us both and said, "I just want to tell you how great a couple you are. You guys have so much powerful, sexual chemistry."

"Thank you," I replied.

One thing I can say about Luna is that she could stand ten feet away and I could still feel her energy. She said the same about me. That is a both a blessing and a curse, I suppose. The blessing is that you can feel each other's vibration and bring each other up. But, when one is down, the other can drag them right into the abyss with them.

Luna spent the weekend prior to the 4th of July with me, as her kids were with their father. During this weekend, I would come to know the greatest intimacy and love-making I have ever felt or taken part in.

I picked her up at her apartment and away we went on a hot summer day to my house. Once there, I told her to make herself comfortable. Apparently, comfortable to her was taking her clothes off and lying naked on the edge of the pool. I made us margaritas, took them outside and had a seat next to her. Needless to say, I couldn't take my eyes off her. The energy between us was like something I had never felt. It was electric and powerful, like two, huge magnets pulling towards each other. I leaned over and gave her a kiss on her beautiful large, perfectly shaped lips and it was on.

We could not keep our eyes, hands or any other body part off each other. Even though I wasn't trying to keep track, I did and we had sex fifteen times that weekend. I've never been able to do it in the pool, but we did. Never been able to do it in the shower, but we did. Never been able to do it in the bathtub, but we did. She told me that she was able to have orgasms we with me that she was never able to before. This of course, made me feel very special. While my ego wanted to believe that she was only this way with me, I had to be realistic and assume that she was like this with other men, as well. Ultimately, I passed it off as just two passionate Scorpios being incredibly, sexually in tune with each other.

After that weekend, we started to see a lot of each other. I was still having conversations with Mye and, to be honest, that was where my heart was. But, Mye could not come here and I could not go there and I was following what I felt was "destiny." Luna bathed me in affection and attention, although I was not convinced that it was totally authentic. I went along with it, though. After all, we were both adults enjoying each other and it was fun.

I thought the fact that she had kids meant there would be no need to get serious quickly. However, two Scorpios together can do nothing slowly. Luna was also a very giving soul. She bought gifts for me and my home. She took me out to eat and bought presents for me to give to my kids. At times, though, I felt like she was trying to buy me and the relationship. I passed this off as her just being a loving, sharing woman. She was not much of a conversationalist and could be quite solemn at times, but Luna was intriguing and a mystery to me and everything was fun and exciting.

Vanished

In August, my daughter was having a big "Back to College" party at my house in the countryside. I asked Luna if she wanted to be part of the event and she said sure. It would be the first time one of my kids would actually meet her. Luna fit in perfectly. She bought my daughter a beautiful necklace for the party and my daughter and her friends got along well with her. She helped me with the cooking and prep work and the constant duties of running a party.

Later in the night, an already passionate Luna wanted to get intimate in one of the bathrooms. Although I was always game to be intimate with her, I had a house full of guests, including my daughter and her boyfriend. I was not comfortable, but she insisted. Soon, as we started to get it on, someone knocked on the bathroom door and we had to stop. I told her we would resume this later, but it was a bad idea right now. I guess she thought I was mad because she started to pout. I told her to not be upset, that it was just not a good time. I walked out to the hammock bed in the yard and lay down. It was a perfect, warm summer night for being outside.

At around two a.m., I awoke to hideous sounds coming from the music room. I approached the door to find two buzzed, college kids trying to play my guitars. I asked them if they had seen Luna and they looked at me like, "Who the hell is Luna?"

I began my search for her in the places where I thought she would most likely be. I started in the bedroom. She wasn't there, so I then searched the kitchen, bathrooms and, lastly, the garage. She was nowhere to be found. Now, I was worried. I had looked everywhere. I called her cell phone, but got no answer. I asked everyone still awake or sober enough if they had seen her, but no one had. I ended up going to bed, wondering where in the hell could she have gone.

Around eight a.m., I felt her slide into bed with me. She smelled fresh and lovely, the way she always did. Luna to me smelled like a beautiful flower and every inch of her being smelled that way to me. She climbed into bed and, before I had a chance to ask her anything, she began "motivating" me down below. The next thing I knew, she was giving little Elvis a tongue bath. When she was done, she put her arms around me and looked at me with a sad, remorseful look, like a child who had done something wrong.

"Where the hell have you been? I couldn't find you anywhere. I called and you didn't answer and I was worried to death."

She looked at me and said, "I thought we had a fight and you didn't want me, so I left."

"Fight? We didn't have a fight!"

"I thought we did and that you were mad at me," she pouted.

"Luna, I live in the country. Where did you go and how did you get there?"

"I went home. I got a taxi to meet me at the VFW down the street because he didn't know where your address was."

"The VFW hall is two and half miles down the road. You walked two and a half miles late at night?"

"Yes."

"What about your kids? Did they know you came home and left again?" I inquired.

"No, they were still asleep."

"How did you get back here?"

"A taxi. It cost almost thirty dollars."

"You are nuts!"

She held me tighter and kissed me on the face, but I let her have it. "I can't trust someone who will get upset about nothing, put herself in danger, go all the way home, which is a half hour away and then, reappear like nothing ever happened."

"Please, Stephen! I thought you didn't want me," she cried.

I told her that after everyone had left, I would take her home and it was over. But, have you ever met someone who was able to convince you of anything? Luna was one of those people.

When everyone woke up and started helping clean the now destroyed house, Luna offered to buy everyone quiche from the restaurant. So, she persuaded me to take her to pick it up and she was the hero of the day. The famished, half-drunk, hung-over college kids happily ate the quiche for breakfast.

Once everyone was gone, we got into the pool. She clasped onto me and we bobbed around the pool, face-to-face. I so enjoyed looking at that beautifully expressive face and holding and kissing her that I softened my demand that we split up. I told her that what had happened last night could never happen again. She agreed and we made peace and love and all was wonderful again. But, in my spirit, I knew it might happen again.

Santa Ynez Wine Trip

In September, I planned to go to Santa Ynez to pick up some wine from the wineries I belong to. Luna couldn't wait to go with me. I picked her up early one bright, warm Saturday morning. We bought a breakfast burrito to share on the way up. She seemed so happy and when Luna was happy, the world could see it. She had that big, sweet smile and a twinkle in her eyes. That was one of the many things that attracted me to her.

With the top down and the iPod blasting AC/DC, all was right with the world. Then, I felt something change inside the car about halfway up to our destination. It was as if the car had been filled with sunshine and light and then, darkness and cold suddenly set in. I looked at her and saw that she was crying.

"What's wrong?" I asked.

"Nothing," she replied.

"Come on, you're crying. Did I do something?"

"No, just drop it. I'm okay, I'm always okay."

That statement I would hear many times during our relationship. It seemed to be her mantra. She was like this for a long period of time and I let it affect me. I was no longer in the same cheerful, happy place we had both started off in. I was so confused about what was happening with her that I missed our exit and had to double back.

Once at the wineries, she seemed to be fine. We each had a tasting, which was a mistake for her, as she got buzzed a little too fast. This resulted in a change in her behavior once more. That same dark cloud once again landed in the passenger seat of my car.

"What happened? Why the dark cloud?" I asked her, as we headed for dinner.

"Pull over."

"We are almost at the restaurant."

"Pull over, now," she demanded.

"No, I will when we get to the restaurant," I insisted.

I knew she was ready to explode, but I was not pulling off the highway. Our destination was just minutes away. Once there, she asked me to open the trunk to the car. I did as she requested. She angrily grabbed her bags and her purse and, in the process, broke a $10 wine glass she had just bought.

"Settle down, what's the matter with you?" I asked.

"I'm walking home."

"Really, you're walking home? We are two and a half hours from home and you're walking? You are crazy."

She walked away as I pleaded with her to stop. I gently grabbed her arm.

"You need to listen to me. This is not funny and you are not walking home. You are either coming in to have dinner with me and behave or you are going to sit your ass in the car and stay there until I come out. Those are your two choices. I am hungry and I know you are, so what are you going to do?"

I felt like a father scolding his young daughter. She reluctantly got back into the car and refused to come in to eat. So, I took my keys and went myself. I'll be damned if I let anyone ruin my trip up to my happiest fucking place on Earth.

I went into the restaurant upset, but hell bent on having a good meal. I was doing just that when she started calling me from the parking lot over and over, but I wouldn't pick up. Then, she came storming through the doors and grabbed my keys.

"You left me in the car to feed your fucking face? Fuck you!" she screamed for everyone to hear.

Then, she stomped out of the room with the keys. I hurried to finish, but again, I was not going to give into this type of manipulative, childish behavior. I have to say, never in my fifty plus years have I ever dealt with or experienced someone like Luna. I've never been with anyone as sexy and alluring and yet, in many ways, so much like a spoiled, angry, little child. Her mood swings and emotional ups and downs had me in knots.

I left the restaurant to see that she had pulled my car up to the handicap zone and was sitting in the driver's seat.

"Luna, please get out," I asked, nicely.

"No, I'm driving," she slurred.

"No, you are not. Now, give me my keys."

"No, I'm driving."

I opened the driver side door.

"Get out of the car, now," I said, firmly

Reluctantly, she got and stumbled around to the passenger side and got in. As I backed out of the lot, I told her that I had it with this type of behavior.

"Stop the car, please," she asked, nicely.

I did as she asked, thinking she wanted to talk to me. Surprisingly, she opened her door and ran away into the night.

What the fuck, I said to myself. I parked the car and got out to search for her, but couldn't find her. Worried, as she seemed capable of doing something crazy, I called the female owner of the restaurant to see if she could call her and calm her down. She agreed to help and when she called, I heard Luna's phone ringing in the car. I got back in the car and circled the block and finally found her. I pulled up and firmly told her to get in the car, as my patience was already sapped. She did and then demanded to be taken home.

"Nope, this is the plan: we go to the motel and we sleep, then head home in the morning," I said.

"Take me home now!" she demanded.

"No, we are going to the motel and I will take you home tomorrow!"

Once at the motel, we walked in, dropped the bags and brushed our teeth. She was pouting and crying and I was frustrated and tired. We climbed into bed.

"I know that you are a good person, but this type behavior is not working for me. You are forty-years-old with kids, how can you act like this?"

She began to cry even louder and she begged me to forgive and love her. When I touched her and told her that I cared about her but I couldn't be in a relationship like this, she broke into a haunting, scary, primal scream. She crumpled to her knees, face down in a fetal position, just sobbing and sobbing. Then, she rolled onto her side and then, onto the floor where she sobbed for at least an hour.

So loud, angry, desperate and violent was her crying that I almost thought about calling a hospital. She wailed and flung herself around until she had nothing left. I pulled her back up to the bed, placed my arms around her and, without a word, tried to make her feel cared about. There was something in her that was badly missing. Was it a lack of unconditional love and affection? Was it the lack of attention or was there something else? Prior drug or alcohol abuse, molestation, physical abuse? I had no way of knowing.

The next morning was like how it feels after a rain storm has moved through. The air felt clean and fresh and things between us seemed renewed. I had not forgotten, nor forgiven what she did the day and night before, but I felt great empathy and understanding for her. She was so lovely and, at the core, she had a good heart, but something bad had happened to cause such pain and sorrow.

I was able to talk to her over the next few weeks about what happened and why she went to the dark side. Turns out, she never really had a secure father figure in her life. She never knew her biological father, who was reported to be a drug addict, and the one she does call Dad took care of her until he and her mother split. At a young age, she lived with her mother, who she says was mean-spirited and sold drugs out of the house. She reported that men were always coming and going, sometimes for drugs, sometimes to visit her mother and sometimes for both. Then, her mother married a man who supposedly abused the whole family, both physically and emotionally.

She also mentioned other male family members who had reportedly molested her and her siblings. I was now seeing a pattern in her that I experienced in my brief relationship with Aracelli: they both seemed to have father issues and abusive, lonesome childhoods.

Now that I understood her troubles, I wondered if my being in her life would make things better or worse. In all of my relationships, my promise to the other person and to myself was to always tell the truth. The truth can hurt, but a lie can be so much more damaging, for after a lie is uncovered, one must question what else the person may have lied about. Could she deal with me being truthful and not saying the things she wanted to hear?

As I wondered what effect I might have on her life, I began thinking about what her presence in my life might do to me. I asked God every night in my prayers what I should do. The answer I got every time was to show her love and to be patient. I had to learn patience over my fifty years, as I had never been good at it. Patience was not a word in my vocabulary when I was younger, but now that I was older, I realized the value and power of the word. With Luna, I was pressed to be patient almost every moment I was with her, as she was emotionally and mentally a loose cannon.

An Embarrassing Moment

One night, her kids had retreated to the two guest rooms in my house when she and I retired to my bedroom. I have an entry door to my room that has no lock. The only way to latch it is to wrap a shoestring or something like that around the knobs of the doors. I was going to do just that when she told me there was no need. Her kids would never burst into the room without knocking.

We started making love and were going at it with me on top of her when I sensed something behind me. I turned to see her son slowly leaving the room as quietly as he had come in. I freaked. Then, I did the dumbest thing I could have done in trying to cover up our deed.

"Okay, I got you Luna! I win the wrestling match," I said loud enough for him to hear it.

Luna looked up at me, confused.

"What the heck are you talking about?"

"Didn't you see him?" I asked, out of breath.

"He who?"

"Your son, he walked in and saw us shagging."

"No, he didn't."

"Yes, I heard someone behind me and when I turned around, he was leaving. You need to get dressed and go talk to him."

"No, he'll be okay."

"No, he won't. You need to get dressed and go talk to the boy because he got a bird's eye view of my ass and my dangling participles and he's bound to be freaking out."

Reluctantly, she did as I asked. About twenty minutes later, she came back and said, "He got up because he was scared of the coyotes outside."

"Okay, that explains why he got up, but why did he just walk in without knocking and what did he say about what he saw?"

She got upset at my question, but I felt that it was a valid one. I was not the perfect father, but I taught my kids you never just burst into other people's rooms without knocking, as that is disrespectful. Now, I understand him being freaked out about the coyotes, but then she told me that he said nothing about seeing what I know he experienced. She said he never brought it up.

I was so afraid to see him the next morning. I mean, what do you say to a young boy who saw you having sex with his mother?

"Hey kid, your mom is hot and what a lay!"

More importantly, why did his mother not get as upset or concerned about what happened as I did? Had this occurred before with other guys? Was this par for the course? All I can say is, to this day, I can laugh about what happened, but, at the same time, feel great embarrassment and empathy for the boy.

In spite of all the chaos of being in a relationship with Luna entailed, we did share some touching, lovely moments together. When she woke up in the morning, she would lay her head on my chest and listen to my heartbeat. I would stroke her gorgeous, jet-black hair as we talked about our dreams and aspirations. After we made love, we'd get up, grab a cup of coffee and go out to the deck to sit in the morning sun. She was so peaceful, loving and gentle that I couldn't help but fall in love with this part her. If only she was like this all the time, then our life together would have been a dream come true.

Birthdays and Holidays / Surgery Time

Between the middle of October and the middle of November, there were five birthdays between our families. We celebrated each and every one. We had a wonderful Thanksgiving with Enrique and his family at my house. There was plenty of food and amazing wine that he brought from the restaurant. Luna made red velvet cupcakes for dessert and we played games until people started falling asleep. Once everyone went home and her kids were tucked in and asleep, Luna and I went to bed. I felt that things were coming together, that even though there were as many question marks to this relationship as there were positives, maybe this could work.

Christmas came and my ex-wife, Jessica, and her partner, Connie, along with our daughter, Brianne, joined us for the festivities. Sadly missing was Michael, who was at college back east and was spending Christmas with parts of Jessica's family. We had a wonderful dinner together and it seemed that Luna, Jessica and Connie all got along well. That was a milestone, as many times, when you try and blend exes with the new family, there is usually hell to pay. When Jessica, Connie and Brianne were leaving, Jessica made the comment, "Stephen, you have a great family here."

It made me smile to think that maybe I did. Luna used to always tell me how much she loved my kids and how she loved them just the same as her own and how she, too, felt we were a family. But, just when it seemed possible, the wheels started to wobble a bit.

I was scheduled to have my left knee replaced on January 11, 2010. The days between New Year's and my surgery were tense between Luna and me for reasons I couldn't immediately grasp. It seemed like she could only wear the mask of happiness for so long. One night, we were having dinner at my house with Asa and Luna's kids when her son put too much food on his plate. Instead of nicely addressing the issue, she ripped into him in front of everyone.

"You're going to eat everything on that plate, you fat, little piggy."

Asa and I were shocked and her son was devastated. I tried to lighten the conversation by saying, "Hey, there's plenty of food. Don't worry about it,"

Luna shot me a look that seemed to say, "I'm going to kill you Stephen."

Asa, who is a wise soul, made a gentle suggestion to the boy.

"Next time, take just a little and if you're still hungry, get a little more, okay?"

The boy nodded. The mood was uncomfortable for the rest of the night. We watched a college football bowl game, but there was tension and frustration in the air. Luna refused to talk to me. One of her daughters sat in a corner away from the TV by herself and refused to join the rest of us. You could cut the tension in the air with a knife and everyone felt it. The only positive thing was that her son leaned against Asa's shoulder and body as they watched the game. His opening up to Asa was a sign that the boy badly needed a male figure and confidant in his life.

Later on that night when discussing my surgery and such, things got even more intense. She requested that I recuperate at her tiny apartment, where I would be on a couch. I told her thanks, but no, I wanted to be in my wonderful Temperpedic bed and at home where I felt comfortable. She demanded otherwise, saying that she could take care of me at her place better since she didn't drive. I told her thanks, but no thanks, I really wanted to be where I felt comfortable and in my own space. Plus, I had my dog. She got angry and hurt, claiming I didn't "need" her. To me, when you need someone or something, you place yourself in the position of lack or of not having what you want. In other words, she needed me to need her in order to feel whole or good about herself. I wanted her, desired her and cared for her, but did not need her. This explanation did not sit well with her or her ego, but I had to concentrate on my health and upcoming surgery, not on her being upset. I had a lot to deal with and would miss one months' worth of work.

That night, as we lay in bed talking, I felt compelled to ask her why she was always so hard on her son.

"He's a good kid," I said.

"Because he reminds me of his worthless, no-good father."

"He's a kid. Why are you comparing him to his dad?"

"Because they are just alike. I see everything in my son that I hate and despise in my ex.

"Luna, you can't do this to your son. Even if he reminds you of the bad things about your ex, you can't punish him for that."

She just stared at me as if what I said meant nothing. I went to sleep with her haunting words in my head and realized that this boy had no chance in hell to ever make her happy or proud.

Many times, when people act out in a negative, emotional way, there could be issues of self-worth or feeling of inadequacy. We all have moments where we don't feel up to the task or comfortable in a situation or crowd we are with. But, Luna seemed to constantly battle with this. She would often say crazy things and ask me strange questions like, "Are you going to leave me? You're going to dump me, aren't you? You're never going to love me."

I assume all of this negativity and lack of security came from her rough family life. One thing I do know is if you say something long enough and believe it to be true, it will become true in your mind. The thoughts we have and the words we speak drive nails into our conscientiousness until we believe it, right or wrong, good or bad. Like Abraham says through Esther and Jerry Hicks, in their book, *The Law of Attraction: The Basics of the Teachings of Abraham.* "A belief is a thought you keep thinking." "A belief is a thought you keep thinking." A belief is a thought you keep thinking."

Somehow, I didn't make her feel convinced about me caring for her and, at the same time, she was draining me of my spirit and well-being with all of her negative questions, actions and mood swings. Nothing I did or said was right or good enough and I couldn't take it anymore. I needed to think of my physical and emotional health heading into surgery the next morning. So, I took drastic action and I broke the relationship off. She was angry and devastated.

The next morning, Asa drove me to the hospital. Luna, although we were technically over with, still requested to be there for me, and I appreciated her doing so. I remember as they were prepping me for surgery, I stared at her and thought she was truly the most beautiful woman I had ever seen and I felt a spiritual, past life connection with her. As I looked at her face, I had a flashback to a time in another life when she and I were making love. She was an Indian woman and was lying on her back with me above her, staring into her eyes and soul. I could not see who I was, but I distinctly saw her eyes, her face and her spirit. We had been together before and I knew it.

"Why do you keep looking at me like that?" she asked me.

"Because you are so amazingly beautiful."

I felt in my heart and soul that we were, at one time, in another life, great lovers, but that, maybe in this life, due to some horrible past life issue between us, it wasn't meant to be.

She and Asa were there when I woke up from the four-hour surgery. They stayed for a while, but it was getting late and Luna needed to get home to take care of her kids.

The next day, they returned and visited with me, but I was pumped up on morphine, so life was a little blurry. Jessica and Connie came to spend time with me, as well, and, for a moment, all were present at one time. Asa and Jessica got into a political debate, which, from my fuzzy state of mind, sounded hilarious. Luna, however, was down and despondent and I know she had a right to be. I had made my decision to call off the romance again, but this time, I was serious. I was feeling her negative energy and it seriously bothered me.

Jessica, having been with me for sixteen years, told her what she needed to do to take care of me. Though misguided as this may be, Jessica still loved me and wanted the best for me. Luna took the advice hard, as she knew that, for all intents and purposes, she was no longer responsible for my well-being. I cared so much for Luna, but her ups and downs were emotionally and psychically were killing me.

Luna's energy was so negative and strong at one point that I looked up at her pouting face and said, "Luna, I am trying to heal here. I know you are upset at me, but you need to stop taking my energy."

There was this cloud of darkness sitting on her shoulders at times, and maybe, because, I have so much empathy and sensitivity to other people's feelings and emotions, I felt it more easily.

She leaned over to me and said, with Jessica and Connie present, "You have so many people who love you, that you don't need me."

She flashed me a sad look and left the room. I can only tell you now, that I felt my energy pick up the moment she left. I felt I needed support and laughter, not sadness and pity.

For all practical purposes, my heart and soul wanted Luna to be "it." I wanted this woman, who scared me, hurt me, loved me, sexed me, cherished me and cursed me to be the one. I felt a deep connection physically and emotionally that I had never really felt before. Also, to be honest, I was tired of dating and being with different women. I wanted and needed to forge a relationship with someone who was unique and special and I felt, in spite of all the craziness with her, that maybe she was it.

Jessica and Connie stayed for about an hour after Luna and Asa left. They made me laugh with remarks and jokes and that was the medicine I needed. As they were leaving, they told me they loved me. No one knows how much that meant to me. I think it speaks volumes that, even though Jessica and I had been through a tough divorce and that Connie was one of the reasons we split up, that later, we could be friends. I appreciated their love and concern for my well-being.

Asa came to take me home after three drug-weary days in the hospital. Upon arriving at my house, I found it to be decorated with balloons, cards, flowers, food and supplies, all courtesy of Luna and her kids. It brought a tear to my eyes. I asked myself how I could have broken up with someone who seemed to care so much for me. Then, I remembered that even though she might have cared for me, I shouldn't forget all the bad stuff that happened.

She never called once to see how I was doing. Yes, I know I broke her heart by calling off the relationship and had no right to expect any communication from her, but on the other hand, if people truly care for each other, wouldn't you want to know how they are? Are emotions and feelings of love so easy to dismiss?

It rained and rained and rained the month I was held up in my house, recuperating. So much so that the dry creek bed below me formed a small river and broke my water pipe. The rain was so torrential that water and mud entered the back of my house through a gap in the door and sent a river of red clay and water into two of the back rooms. It must have been quite a sight to see me trying, with one leg, to sop up the water and slime and seal off the back door.

Enrique came to the rescue by reattaching my pipe and grading my washed-out road so that people could come and see me. Asa, Enrique, Rosa and my brother, Dino, kept me stocked with food and supplies. My good friend, Dee, came up to fix me dinner, as did my friend, Gabby. I had so many people helping me that I was awestruck. You never know your friends and what they are made of until you need them. Luna, however, was still MIA.

The rain and cold of January and February seemed to fit my mood. I was so pumped up on pain killers that I rarely ate. I didn't feel like watching TV, writing, reading, drinking wine or anything. The only thing I desired was sleep and meditation. It was an important moment in my life. I felt I was becoming more removed from what you might call the normal routine and pleasures of life. I was happy and yet, alone.

I was told by a friend who had a massive injury and was on pain killers for a long time that it is the effect of the drugs on you that causes this feeling of falling into an abyss. He said it was not enlightenment, but drugs. I think for me, it was a combination of both.

One thing was for sure, I never stopped thinking about two people: Luna and Mye. Being with Mye, however, was impossible. We had given up on ever being together and she was angry and frustrated by that. I spoke to her a couple of times when I was recuperating, only to have her tell me she had a woman lover because she could never imagine being with another man after me. She said I broke her heart and that another man could never have it. I felt helpless and frustrated over that statement, but there was nothing I could do. We agreed to never talk again and so, painfully, Mye was now forever lost.

But, with Luna, I always felt there might be a chance of reconciling things if she would admit and agree to therapy and counseling. She had some deep-seeded anger issues that needed to be uncovered and released. Somehow, I was quite adept at pushing those buttons and bringing her anger to the forefront.

I remember just how angry I had made her back in October 2009. We attended one of my account's wine festivals at the old Saugus race track. We met up with friends and had a great time perusing the various wineries and food vendors. There was a live band, which we caught near the end of the event, but we danced and had fun while we could. When the band finished, they put on music and started to escort people out.

We got to my car and a song by Jennifer Lopez came on the event PA system.

"Let's go back and dance," Luna said.

"No, we can't, babe. They are chasing people out."

"I want to dance!" she demanded.

Now, when she started to get like this, especially after drinking, I would get quiet to try and keep the peace. However, that night, I didn't feel inclined to take that path.

"You can dance when we get home," I said.

"No, I want to dance now!" she said, as she got back out of the car.

"Luna, we are leaving."

Reluctantly she got back in the car and the darkness set in. I turned on some music on the radio as we drove away, hoping it might calm her down. Then, she muttered something about me being controlling by not letting her go back and dance.

"I don't know what it is about dancing. It's a primitive action, much like sex. All people are born with the desire to dance," I said.

She took offense to that.

"You're saying everyone can dance?" she barked.

"No, what I am saying is, if you ever watch a little kid and somebody puts on music, they start to dance. It's primitive, lower chakra energy, much like our need for sex, eating and survival."

"How dare you say it's primitive!"

"I'm not saying there's anything wrong with it, but it is what it is. In theory, anyone can dance."

That was it. She angrily turned off my car stereo. I turned it back on and she turned it off again. I decided to shut up and let it go.

Upon reaching my place that she and others called "The Oasis", she began to tell me what an arrogant ass I was for saying everyone could dance. Notice, I did not say everyone could dance well, but that everyone can dance, depending on your technical opinion of the subject. She then turned to me in the master bath and said something that today, still makes me laugh.

"Goddamn it, Stephen, I'm a dancer!" she cried out, with a scowl on her face.

"Baby, I'm sure you are," I said, calmly, as I walked out of the bathroom and into my bedroom.

Then, she went berserk. She felt her swimsuit hanging on the towel rack in the bathroom.

"Who's been using my swimsuit?" she screamed.

"What are you talking about?"

"Who's been using my swimsuit? It's still wet"

"Maybe it's still wet from last weekend."

"Who have you had up here? Who's been wearing my suit?" she said, as she threw it to the floor.

"No one has been here, Luna. Settle down."

She then flew out of the bathroom towards me.

"I don't trust you. I talked to your friends and they say you always have someone up here!"

The reality of the situation is that when I am with one woman, I am with one woman. I do not cheat or do anything to betray their trust. You could ask my exes, Mary or Jessica, and they would tell you that. But, Luna was in a tornado of emotions and she was beginning to get violent. She suddenly pushed me.

"No one has been here and stop pushing me," I told her, firmly.

She then grabbed something off my dresser and threw it at me. It hit me in the right shoulder and then, swung her fist at me. I grabbed her arm and said, "I don't do this. I don't fight and I don't hit."

Then, I told her to get her shit, that I was taking her home and it was over again. Then she started to pout and cry and ask for forgiveness.

Have you noticed a pattern regarding my threats to take her home and say goodbye? From Santa Ynez wine tasting to now, I rarely followed through and I was inconsistent with my threats. She would always calm down and, like the typical, abusive relationship, she would sugarcoat everything and apologize to the point of reconciliation. I've never been addicted to anything, but somehow, I felt addicted to her.

So, now, cut back to me, lying in bed with my knee swollen to the size of a grapefruit. I thought of her and how amazing she would be if she would only "work on" herself. Well, I decided that she needed some help and just maybe, superhuman Stephen could do the job. I convinced myself that I had not really tried before and that I was just mostly reacting negatively towards her strange behaviors.

Luna (Part Two)

We had begun some small conversations when I returned to work in February. After all, I saw her every Monday when I went to the restaurant to do their order. Not knowing where we stood, but still respecting her, I bought her roses, chocolate and a bottle of wine for Valentine's Day, which she tossed in the trash because the roses were yellow. I was a little hurt, but understood. She's an emotional person who wanted red roses, which represent love and passion, not yellow ones that represent friendship. But, I wanted to see if we could forge a friendship first and then, reinvestigate the romantic side of things.

She would call me sometimes and we would chat. Interestingly, we could talk and talk for long periods of time when not together as a couple. Sometime in March, she asked me if I would take her to the store and I said yes because she still couldn't drive. Clad in her wait staff uniform, I picked her up at the restaurant and I took her shopping. Since we were together, I asked her if she wanted me to make dinner and she told me yes.

At my house, we opened a bottle of wine and sat on the edge of the pool talking. I was absolutely mesmerized by her. Then, I felt like I had to make a confession. I told her that because I was still crazy about Mye, maybe I had not given Luna and us a fair shake. She told me her woman's intuition told her that I was never completely in the relationship with her. She always did accuse me of being one foot in and one foot out, which was true. But, the reason I was never fully in, was not completely because of Mye; it was because I wasn't sure I trusted Luna or believed she really, truly loved me. I never could put my finger on why, but my gut told me that she acted this way with most men she was with. However, there was a plausible possibility if I was to give her all of me this time, just maybe she would be different. Leopards do change their spots, right?

It was kind of funny, but I never knew which Luna I was going to be with on a date with her: Jekyll, Hyde or both? Hey, I admit it. There's something sexy and intriguing about someone you can't quite figure out. Her being Sybil caused me to be interested, but not want to plan or build anything long-term with her.

This time, I told her I would commit to the relationship if she worked on being happy and get therapy. She explained that she had been to meditation classes and that was working wonders with her issues. She also told me that she found a real therapist who was helping her. For some reason, I believed her.

We got back together and initially, everything was really wonderful. She seemed to be authentically happy and the therapy and meditation seemed to be working.

In May, her kids and I attended Enrique's big Memorial Day party at his home. It was like a scene out of a European movie: a beautiful park-like yard, surrounded by grapevines, kids running everywhere and people speaking French, Spanish and English. There was plenty of food, wine and people of all ages, backgrounds and ethnicities.

While her kids met up with some other kids at the party and were doing their thing, Luna and I stayed glued to each other. We had some amazing BBQ and great wine and the day was perfect.

While chatting with an old woman sitting at a table outdoors, she instructed me to take off my hat, which I did. She saw my bald head and told me I looked much better without the silly hat. As I continued to talk to the woman, Luna drifted off into the house.

When I walked into the house a few minutes later, I saw that she was consuming a liquor drink Enrique had prepared. She is not a good drinker and so mixing whatever it was with hours of drinking wine was not a smart idea. I told her to be careful.

"I'm fine, I'm not a kid," she said.

Soon, I saw her with yet another fresh drink.

"Luna, you shouldn't be mixing drinks, you're going to get sick," I whispered to her.

She angrily turned to me in front of friends and said, "You are not my father, leave me alone."

I dreaded what I knew was going to happen. I walked outside and talked to a couple that owned a restaurant down the street. They invited us to a 4th of July party at their house that I accepted. As we talked about the restaurant business and the challenging economy, Rosa's daughter, Celina, came out to find me. She told me to hurry and come inside. Her tone seemed urgent and troubled. As I walked into the house, Rosa, Enrique's wife, was pointing at something in the kitchen. There, to my disbelief, was Luna kicking their new dishwasher.

"Luna what are you doing?" I asked her.

"The fucking thing won't shut," she slurred.

I took the handle and shut the door easily. She stumbled off back towards the bar as Asa pulled me aside.

"She's drunk. You need to take her home and now!" he advised.

Enrique, in the meantime, had put on dance music and Luna was one of the first to jump at that. As she danced, I went to round up her kids so we could leave. Once I found them, I had them sit at the bar in the kitchen, where they saw everything unfolding. Luna had secured yet another drink and was bumping and grinding Claude, the gay maître d. When the song ended, I hurriedly went to her.

"Come on, babe. We are leaving."

She glared at me with hazy eyes and a look that would kill.

"I'm not going," she loudly slurred.

Then, Asa and Enrique approached us.

"Luna, you're drunk. Stephen needs to take you home," Asa said.

"It's time to go," Enrique added, softly.

"OK, let's go," I tell her.

She turned and loudly, drunkenly announced, to her kids and everyone there, "You heard it, King Stephen has spoken. Kids go get in the car!"

She stormed out of the door in a huff with the kids in tow. I apologized to all my friends and went out to the SUV, where I knew either an ambush or morgue was waiting. It ended up being a little of both.

It was silent as we drove the four miles down the street to my house to get their stuff before taking them home. I had noticed at the party that her son, who was always surrounded by three females and high estrogen levels, had been playing video games with the boys. In trying to lighten things up, I asked him what video games he had been playing.

As he started to answer, some of the meanest words ever spoken flew out of his mother's mouth.

"Don't answer him. He doesn't give a fuck about you!"

I looked at his face in the rearview mirror and saw it drop. I tried to repair the harsh words.

"She's wrong, I do care about you."

Luna stayed in the SUV as I led her kids in to get their belongings. As they waited for me to unlock the door, I turned and hugged each one of them and said, "It's going to be OK."

The truth was that I doubted my own words. After gathering their stuff, we headed off to her apartment. Luna was silent the whole way home because she had passed out. Her kids did not utter a single sound and I felt for them.

I pondered whether or not she had done this before with other guys. With regard to other men in her life, I know for a fact, when I asked her out in January of 2009 and she refused me, it was because she was dating a guy. But, the time she asked me to take her to the Wine Festival in June, the guy she broke up with was someone different. So, to these kids, I was at least the third man they had been introduced to in less than a year. I wondered how they must feel about her, me and us.

When we arrived at her apartment, I asked one of her daughters to get the key from her mother's purse. No way was I going digging around in there. Once the key was found, I asked them to go brush their teeth and get ready for bed, as they had school the next day. They were great kids and did exactly as I asked.

In the meantime, I had to figure out how to get Luna, who was out like a light, up a flight of stairs. I went to grab her out of the passenger's seat and I wrapped my arms tight around her. As I pulled her slowly out of the car, she felt like a dead body. She started to slip through my grip and onto the grass below. There, I plead with her to help me help her.

Just as I was asking, she threw up on herself. I moved her out of the mess and she threw up again. Luckily, a woman was passing by her apartment and asked me if I needed help.

"Yes, please," I responded.

The woman's name was Angel and talk about a blessing. She was a large, strong Hispanic woman and she helped me carry Luna up the stairs and into the bathroom. Once she was seated on the toilet, Luna began to moan and cry, much like she did the time in the motel room when we were wine tasting. Angel stayed with her the whole time as Luna wept and screamed horrible things to and about me, in front of her kids. I watched their faces, as these words and violence permeated us all. They came and sat down next to me in the hallway and I began to cry. We all were crying. Then, I asked her son a stupid question.

"Does she get this way with other guys or your dad?"

"No, only with you."

My heart sunk like a stone to my stomach.

"Only with me?"

"Well, she did this a couple of times when you were broken up," he added.

"Who helped her then?"

"The owners of the restaurant."

I know I'm a good, caring person, I thought to myself. Surely, I could not have caused all this. What role or part did I play in this scenario? And, "Aye, there lies the rub", as Shakespeare would say.

I began to feel that people like her do these kinds of things unconsciously, to keep you feeling like you owe them, that you are the root of their issues and problems and not them. Therefore, you need to do even more for them. These are the people that suck your soul and energy right out of your body and you know it's happening, but you still allow it or at least try to deal with it.

After Angel and I got her to sleep, we made sure that the kids had both our numbers to call us should something happen. Angel lived across the street, so the kids could knock on her door, if push came to shove.

Around two in the morning, I got a call from Luna.

"Why didn't you stay with me?" she angrily asked, still slurring her words.

"Luna, go to sleep. We will talk about this later," I replied, softly.

"What happened to me?"

"You got drunk. Now, let's talk in the morning."

She agreed and hung up. The next day, she tried to go to work, but couldn't do it, so she went back home. Over the next few days, we spoke about what happened and the horrible things she said to her son and me. The sad thing was that she never took any blame or said that she was sorry. She never admitted that she messed up or was in some way responsible for what happened. She only tried to use her being drunk as some form of immunity.

"Getting drunk and being a jerk speaks of who you really are. Alcohol is a truth serum. It does not make us do anything we are not already capable of," I told her.

All of us have seen happy, funny drunks, depressing drunks and violent drunks. Whether it's alcohol or drugs, these things are simply windows or doors to what is already residing inside the person and this was a woman who was hurt, frustrated and unhappy.

We had one more date that was a disaster the following weekend when we went to the Hollywood Bowl with friends. It was a warm day and we were sitting in the sun. She started to get a little wine buzz.

"Babe, try drinking a glass of water between each glass of wine. You need to stay hydrated."

Luna was into a healthy lifestyle and working out, so she was aware of the need to stay hydrated. She was a runner and did yoga twice a week. But, she took offense at my suggestion and she immediately went dark. I could always feel the steam building up inside her and an explosion was imminent.

Later, when George Benson came to the stage, she wanted to dance, so she headed down to the walkway below us to dance with whoever would take her up on it. As good looking as she was, numerous men immediately flocked to her. My friend, Gary, was concerned and slid over next to me to tell me we should leave soon, especially if things got a little weird.

Once the last song was over, I told her it was time to go. All of us, after eight hours of being in the sun, wanted to leave. She refused, but I convinced her to go. We got into the shuttle and she sat a few rows behind, glaring at me. Gary told me he was concerned and to call him when I got home to make sure everything was okay.

After we got into the car, I told her that this behavior was not working for me and I couldn't take it anymore. She looked at me and mumbled, "I hate you."

I worked so hard to not lose my temper and stay grounded, but I completely lost it. So badly, that I couldn't stop the four letter, horrible words that were flowing from my mouth. I called her things I would never call anyone, but she had dug so deeply into my emotions and psyche that I almost blacked out with anger. I was so upset that I missed our freeway interchange and spent twenty minutes trying to get back.

We spent a tense night together and, in the morning, I apologized to her for everything I said. I even started crying because this was not me.

"I don't do things like this," I told her.

I held her tight as tears rolled down my face and onto her beautiful, brown shoulders. I was embarrassed and ashamed of myself, as no guru or yogi would ever allow himself or herself to become so affected. I was so ashamed of myself and of the negativity she brought out in me that I broke it off yet again.

I had to look inside myself to find where my own anger came from and how I could not only learn from it, but also never let it surface again. I got back into meditation to search for answers.

So, with Luna gone again, I went about living my life. I didn't feel like dating, though months after our breakup I did go out on a few random dates. I definitely did not feel like having sex or being intimate with anyone. That's one of the things about people like her. On the dark side, they steal your spirit and break your will. They can suck you dry of desires and dreams because they want control and to be the only desire and dream that you possess and they don't want any competition. On the bright side, they stroke your ego, smother you with affection, albeit, mostly as an acting job, and make sex and intimacy with them hard to live without. They create a void inside you where you feel, in some sick way, – and I hate to admit it – you need to have them in your life.

After her, no sex was my motto and I held to it. However, Luna needing to feel good, as Halle Berry would repeat again and again in "Monsters Ball", was Luna's mantra as well. "Make me feel good, make me feel good" led her to shag a local musician by the name of Marcus, who already had a rich girlfriend who supported him. I suppose it went like the old saying, when the cat is away, the mice would play. He did just that and Luna became one of his temporary play toys. After knowing her for only a few weeks, Marcus asked her to marry him, only to rescind the offer and go back to his girlfriend a few days later.

I felt pity for her that she was so gullible or stupid. I believed in my heart that I had to let her know my feelings and, on Thanksgiving Day, I let her have it. No holds barred.

I told her what a despicable mess she was and how she was destroying her kids by introducing man after man into their lives. She also accused me a dating a lot of women and she was right. However, there was a major distinction. My kids, when they were young, never met any of my dates unless I had been with them for at least 3-6 months. Also, my kids were older and not present when I was dating these women. Luna was one of the first they met and, by then, they were 18 and 22.

I ended my rant by telling her she needed serious, psychological help. Later, I felt remorse for what I said.

Maybe she only heard the harsh, horrible words and not the love, passion and concern behind them. I could only pray that some of what I had said to her might sink in, that it might make her see the stupidity of the things she had done and was doing to herself and her kids.

I came back from Thanksgiving at my ex-wife's family's place and I let the guilt get to me. I decided to drop off some candy, wine and food to Luna. After all, she was alone on Thanksgiving, a holiday she and I both loved. She was sitting on the steps of her apartment when I arrived.

"How could you ever say those things to me?" she immediately asked.

"Because, crazy as it may sound, I love you Luna. I know where you have been in life and you are repeating the same behavior over and over again looking for a different result and it won't happen."

"My life is none of your business, Stephen. You don't want me, remember?"

"I do want you, Luna, but you continue to sabotage the relationship with your negative behavior and actions. Sometimes, babe, I question your sanity. What does it say about you and your mental stability when your own co-workers are laughing at you behind your back because you entertained marrying a guy you've known for less than a month? A guy who's already involved with someone that supports him and whom he will never leave? How is it everyone else sees and knows how messed up that is but you?"

She only looked at me as if nothing I said had any impact, as if she already knew it and couldn't care less. I told her I was sorry I had to get so graphic and angry, but I felt I needed to say something or regret it forever.

To be honest, I also was not done with her in my heart and I couldn't stand the fact that she was already onto someone else. Yes, I know some might call it ego, but I discovered that, in some sick and possessed way, I really loved her after all. I know some of you would ask how and I would be inclined to ask the same question, but there was some powerful – even sick – connection between us.

When you love someone, you want the best for them, right? Imagine someone you love dearly, maybe your significant other or a son or daughter and you see them headed for trouble. What do you do? Just watch and, when they are in dire straits, say I told you so? Or, do you try your best to protect them from ever getting to that place of regret?

I guess I was arrogant enough to try to prevent what I knew was her destiny. What about her kids? They were not only beautiful children, but I felt extremely con-nected to them, even though they rarely spoke to me. Now, I know why they never talked or invested energy into getting to know me. I was just another guy in a long line of guys. I just happened to be around a little longer than some and I know they were thinking: don't get too close to Stephen; he, too, will soon be history.

Luna (Part Three)

After the blow out on Thanks-giving, I was meditating one night and asked God to help me either get over her or help me help her. The next morning, I was reading *Man's Eternal Quest* by Paramahansa Yogananda and it hit me. There was a chapter about being bigger than the problems or the people around you and that a true Guru and seeker of God could allow things to happen and not be affected by them. It was about allowing people – even mean or obnoxious ones – to be who they are and that, by being peaceful and God-like around them, you would strengthen your connection to the Almighty and have a lasting influence on others, as well.

I let her affect me the first two times and I failed to be the proper spiritual person in her life and, in a way, my own. Super Stephen was going to try again, as he had the power of God and Yogananda behind him.

This was a challenge not only to help her, but for me to truly start showing the love and faith I had in myself and in her. I realized, for whatever reason, that I loved this complete mess of a woman.

California has a three strikes law. Three crimes in a certain period of time equates to a long time in jail or prison. I was down to my last strike to make this work, and for the love of God, I was going to try.

During the first week of December, and after almost six months of not being together, I went to her to her apartment, armed with a bowl of soup I had made her. She was very sick at the time and had taken a day off work to recover. As she ate the soup, I looked her in the eye and asked her, "Do you really, truly love me?"

"Yes, more than any man I have ever known."

"I love you, as well, and I want to try this one more time. But, here is the caveat: if you feel it isn't working, you will have to do the nasty deed and pull the trigger."

"Why do you want to come back Stephen?" she asked.

"Because I can't imagine not seeing your beautiful face every night when I go to bed and every morning when I wake up."

She smiled, hugged me and started to cry. She also told me that she once again had sought and was receiving therapy, as well as doing yoga/meditation classes again to heal her anger with her mother, step-father and herself. She admitted that she needed help. I was excited to hear this, as it showed me she was aware of her problems and maybe, with much practice and support, she could turn the corner on a new way of life.

She also asked me to help with her kids, as she had been a single parent for far too long.

"I don't want to have to be the bad guy all the time," she confessed. "Can you help me?"

"If you will let me, I will Luna. I will."

To keep things uncomplicated, we agreed to keep sex out of the equation, as that was a major attraction, and yet, possibly something that clouded everything else. We were able to last about two weeks before the desires arose and we consummated our third attempt at the relationship.

This time around was different from the first two times together. She held me at arms distance, and said that I needed to prove to her that I really loved and wanted her before she could let me all the way back in. Realistically, it was her that needed to prove something, as it was her blow-ups, anger and dissatisfaction with everything that caused the prior two breakups. But, I needed to accept responsibility, as well, and take the high road.

A funny, yet a poignant expression of who she is happened quickly after we started round three of our relationship. I took her to the store and, while trying to turn into the parking lot, a large SUV that seemed to be the size of a house, was in front of us. The woman driving took so long to turn that it left us in stuck in the middle of the road. Those who know my sense of humor would think nothing of what I muttered, "Come on, butthead, turn."

Luna looked at me and said, "Why can't you have compassion for people?"

I just smiled. I was not going to get into it. She clearly didn't understand that I was just being cheeky.

As we pulled up to the parking stall in my convertible, a woman in front of us was loading things into her car. The woman looked at me and then, gave a long glance to Luna. Out of the blue, and without any inhibition, Luna suddenly called out, "What are you looking at, bitch? I know I am prettier than you!"

I started to laugh.

"So, was that compassion?" I asked.

It was so weird she would step both feet into the same poop she had just warned me about.

Friends of mine saw the two of us together as two very different personalities. They noticed she seemed dark and a little intimidated at times by my friends and me. They often remarked how, when I was having fun and being goofy, she seemed removed, dejected and almost out of place. My pals, who are never short of saying what they truly feel, believed that she was envious and frustrated by me. Luna did say that her friends told her that I was different from the men she had dated before and she needed to understand that.

She used to call me the Sun and herself the Moon. Read the tarot descriptions of those two cards and you would find direct opposite spectrums of life. Even the places we live were opposite, in terms of our personalities. My place is painted in white, gold and yellow. Her place featured dark blues, grays and browns. Colors represent a persons internal view of life and themselves. And, like the old saying goes, opposites attract.

One night, we were talking and she told me the thing she wanted most was to marry and have a complete family again. She said that it was only right the kids should have a father figure in their lives. It was hard to disagree with that. I never contemplated or wanted to get married again, but she was right about the solid father figure bit. This wish was in direct opposition of what she had been showing her kids so far, with the revolving door of relationships she had entertained.

So, one night, I meditated and asked the heavens, should I marry Luna? Now, I know most of you are saying, "WTF? Are you nuts? Dude, look at the past to see what the future looks like and you are setting yourself up for a life of hell." And, you might even be right in those assumptions. But, I felt like I needed to do this, so I bucked up and ordered an engagement ring for her.

I only told a select few of friends about our engagement. When they questioned my sanity, I could only say that I loved her and the kids and that I needed to make it work.

I decided to give it everything I had because unless you put all your heart and effort into something, how can you ever tell if the result was the one it should have been? I also had a theory that if I gave her my heart and provided everything she ever wanted, she would not feel worthy of accepting it and would sabotage it.

On December 30, two days before New Year's, in front of her kids, both of my brothers and Asa, I asked her to marry me. She looked at me with tears in her eye as I presented the ring and she said yes. All three of her kids, who were sitting on the living room sofa, looked up in amazement. Her son came up to the dining table with a big smile on his face and danced around in excitement. The two girls sat on the couch, stunned, and began to cry.

My brothers and Asa congratulated us, although I knew everyone was against it. I hugged her son and then, approached her daughters. I kneeled down to them before speaking.

"I want you to know that I love you and I will not be leaving this time."

I was crying and they were crying. A sob fest was in session. The girls nodded their heads that they were okay, but surprised by the moment. Again, only time would tell.

I told Luna there was no rush to move from her apartment, as the kids were in school until May the following year. She was, however, thrilled with the prospect of living with me, gave notice on her apartment and had to be out by March 1.

"Wow," I said, "are you sure you want to move this fast?"

"Yes, Stephen, I am," she responded, confidently.

"Well, we have a lot to do."

I started cleaning out the two bedrooms that had once been my kids. Her son would have Michael's room and her daughters would share Brianne's larger bedroom. I took things down to the shed and threw away many unneeded items. Luna liked to bake, or at least used to, so I cleaned out numerous counters and cabinets to make room for her things.

In the meantime, she was selling and giving away tables, lamps, furniture and the like at her place to get ready for the upcoming relocation. We still had one problem to solve and that was her lack of transportation. Over the years, she had accumulated speeding tickets and other moving violations, some of which went to warrant. I have to admit this was a sore spot with me, as it made me question her responsibility. Months prior, she had hired an attorney who, one by one, was getting the tickets resolved, in an effort to get her license back. Now, as we planned the move, we not only needed the van to haul things, but she needed to be able to take the kids to school and herself to work, which was twenty-five minutes away. Before that, she and her kids had the luxury of walking to work and school that were only blocks from their apartment.

She called me one day, excited that the tickets were paid and that she got a temporary driver's license. I was thrilled to hear this, so I got busy trying to get the van running. Her boss helped me get the vehicle towed to his mechanic a few blocks away. I went with him back to the restaurant to tell her all was well and the van was in the shop. Luna walked up to me and said, "No one has ever taken such initiative to do something like this for me."

She hugged and kissed me and I felt ten feet tall. Sometimes, all a man needs is to feel appreciated, respected and loved. We are very simple creatures, we men.

A day later, the mechanic called to say $1100 worth of work needed to be done to the van. That seemed high to me, so I called my own mechanic and he told me the work should cost closer to $850. I was able to get the shop to accept that amount, but even then, I knew she didn't have that kind of money. I told her she could put it on my credit card and pay it off when her taxes came back in a few weeks. She refused that arrangement.

"It's not your problem and I don't want to owe you money."

"It was only going to be a few weeks. You can pay it off before I get any interest charges," I said.

"I don't use credit cards, Stephen and I will pay cash for it. I just wished you hadn't rushed it until my taxes came back."

Now, I was really confused. We needed the van to start moving stuff and just the day before, she had thanked me for what I did and now, she's mad at me for the very same thing?

So, we got the van repaired and made a trip to AAA to put it in my name to get it insured. I paid for the transfer and license, as it would be years before her driving record would show any improvement. I had the van smog checked and then, we got the tags. Now, she had a van that was running and, most importantly, FREEDOM! I thought I was doing the right thing for the woman I loved.

Towards the end of January, we looked at colors to paint the kids' rooms. I also began working on the garage/music room to convert it into a guest room for my brother, who was staying with me part time. We talked about getting the girls new beds and replacing the small couches I had with larger sleeper sofas. We went to a couple of furniture stores, looking for what might best fit the new family.

After shopping, we went to have appetizers and drinks and she demanded to pay the bill. To her credit and fault, she was never cheap or selfish with money. When the bill came, it was $70. A good tip in anyone's books would be $14-$16, but she tipped $40. When we got in the car, I had to tell her, "Luna, I know you like to tip, but over 50% is crazy, baby. I know you don't have the money to do things like that."

I brought this up was because I had seen a past due electric bill on the counter of her apartment. It was threatening to turn off her power if not paid in ten days. I had also heard rumors about her spending habits. Her friends had told me that, although she shared her money freely, many times, she would buy things or spend money on herself, even when the rent was late.

I knew why she did this. When you grow up the way she did, you are told you are not worth anything and that you don't deserve anything nice. She bought herself gifts to remind herself that she was worthy. So, when I brought up the tipping issue, I saw the hurricane coming because I had challenged her. Plus, it didn't help that she had two martinis and a beer.

As I drove her back to her place, she became angry. Somehow, the conversation escalated to talking about Marcus, the guy she dated between our last break-up. I got a little unnerved, but I was trying my best to emulate the Buddha/guru life of controlling emotions and reactions. The next thing I know, she was yelling and very upset. Instead of getting immersed and angry in what was being said about me, I faced the steering wheel of my car, took a breath and stayed calm, all the while, listening to her rant and rave. Finally she screamed, "Do you hear me?"

"Yes," I calmly responded.

"Why the fuck are you not saying anything?" she demanded.

"I am letting you express yourself and there is nothing I can say."

"I am talking to you and you're not listening to me. Why won't you talk to me!"

Then, out of the blue, she pushed me and hit me in the side of the face with her fist. I turned, and said, politely, "Please get out of the car."

She just glared and me.

"Luna, please get out of my car."

"Fuck you!" she yelled, as she got out and slammed the door as hard as she could. Then, she stood on the grass in front of her apartment and screamed.

"I hate you, Stephen Hemmert. I fucking hate you, I hate you."

She turned quickly and, without much grace, headed upstairs.

A few weeks later, I noticed a lack of energy in her. Fading was the excitement of moving in and the possibility of changing her life. I wondered if someone else was interfering with her desire to be with me or if, like my prediction had said, she was sabotaging the move because of her insecurities. Then, something completely different and unexpected happened.

Having supposedly settled her traffic tickets and warrants, she got her driver's license back. But, out of the blue, two CHP officers showed up to arrest her at the restaurant. When I asked her why, she said that something on a ticket was not satisfied and that she or her attorney failed to appear in court to take care of it.

How can she have her license back and yet, the DMV, which knows everything, didn't know she had an outstanding ticket and a warrant out for her arrest, I asked myself.

Something didn't make sense. I realized that I never did actually see her new license and now, I started to think that she had lied about getting her license back.

When I first met her, she told me she received an "on the cell phone" ticket by the CHP, but the person recording the ticket information in the system accidentally typed in two DUI codes, as well. Again, I never saw the physical ticket, so I had no idea what it was for. She explained that the attorney was going to court to get the ticket corrected to read just the "on the cell phone" citation. After her court date, she called to say the DUI charges, (erroneous, of course) had been removed and only the cell phone ticket had to be dealt with. I was relieved to know that she didn't really have a DUI because that is serious business.

It was Super Bowl weekend and only a month before she and the kids were to move in with me. I felt compelled to inquire a little more about this mystery ticket and subsequent warrant. She and I were about to blend our lives together, so I should know what was going on, right? I asked her how things had gotten to this point where she was almost arrested and she told me her attorney or someone had messed up. Now, she had to pay another $1,200 to take care of this "mix up." I love her, but something didn't make sense and I didn't buy her explanation.

"Baby, why didn't you take care of the tickets when they happened instead of waiting until they incurred penalties and went to warrant?"

There was silence and then, she went berserk.

"I'm a single mother of three kids and I didn't have the money!" she screamed.

"I understand, but you told me the owners of the restaurant and your dad helped you out from time to time. Why didn't you ask them to help you? Now, this $140 ticket is costing you $1,200."

"Listen, Stephen, I don't need you second guessing me and I don't need your judgment."

"I'm not judging you, I am simply asking a–"

Before I could finish, she hung up on me. My mind was still trying to wrap itself around this whole mess and to me, she was not telling the complete truth.

When she calmed down, she called and asked what my plans were for the day.

"I'm pulling everything out of the music/garage room to make my brother a guest room."

"Well, the kids and I were going to come up, but since you're busy, we won't."

"No, please come. I could really use your help."

Reluctantly, she came up alone. When she arrived, she had the look of disengagement. I picked up on it and asked what was wrong.

"Nothing. What needs to be done?" she asked.

"Well, I need to pull the freezer out, as well as all the workout equipment and the music stuff. Maybe you could box up things to take to the shed."

She just looked at me with absolutely no expression. Then, she walked over and propped herself up on the short retaining wall near where I was working. She looked uncomfortable, so I went and got her a lawn chair to sit in. Moments later, she was asleep. I didn't know what was going on, but I knew somehow I was losing her.

She woke up about thirty minutes later, went directly to the bedroom and fell asleep again. After an hour or two, she came out.

"I want to get the kids and go to Trader Joe's. When are you going to be done?"

"Well, I would have been long ago if you had helped me," I joked with her.

"I was tired."

"I saw that."

Nonetheless, we got into her van and went to Trader Joe's, then picked up her kids. It was the first time we were all in the van together as a potential family.

Back at the house, she and I made dinner for everyone and then, watched a movie. Later, we retired to bed and made love, which was always wonderful, but that time, something felt different. The chemistry was still there, but the excitement that she always showed was MIA.

The next morning was Super Bowl Sunday and she told me how excited her son was about getting to watch the game with my brother and me. When Dino showed up to the house, she made everyone breakfast and then, we packed up more items to put into storage. We did a little work and, of course, retired to the bedroom for a little R&R when the most amazing thing happened. She fell asleep on top of me with me still inside her. I also nodded off and woke up with her still on top of me with her arms wrapped around me. In all my years of love-making and being intimate, this had never happened to me. It was like our two bodies and souls were welded together.

Finally, she awoke and slowly pulled herself off me and headed to the rest room. It was winter and a little chilly in the house.

"I hate your home," she suddenly said.

"You always told me what an amazingly warm, peaceful spiritual place this was and now you hate it?"

Then, she started being even more negative.

"The house isn't big enough for us. This house will never really be mine; it's got your signature and vibe all over it. There's no room for my baking stuff. I've never lived with a man, they always moved in with me."

"But, you were married twice before. Are you telling me you never moved into their place?"

"No, they always lived with me and I don't know if I am comfortable moving into your home."

This negativity was always present, but now, it was an ever-growing trend. Nights before, she called me distraught and when I asked her why she was upset, she said, "We don't have a song."

"A what?"

"A song, we don't have a song."

"Luna, what are you talking about?"

"My ex-husband and I had a song that was special to both of us. A song that speaks of our relationship and love for each other," she explained.

I was dumbstruck, but I thought, Okay, this is important to her.

"Let me meditate about it and I will call you if a song hits me," I offered.

We liked many of the same artists, so I meditated as promised and the song that popped into my head was Corinne Bailey Rae's, "Just like a Star." I called her and she exclaimed with excitement, "That's it!"

As the day went on, Luna got increasingly negative about almost everything. She claimed I never listened to her music, liked what she liked and many other off-the-wall, divisive things. That's when I pulled her back into the bedroom.

"If you want to back out of this, then you are going to have to do it. I made a promise to you and the kids I was not breaking up this relationship. So, this time, if you are not happy or have doubts, it's up to you."

She frowned and said nothing. There was something else was bugging me about the way she was acting. She kept texting someone and since she has few friends and her kids were here in the house, I suspected it was a man.

"Does Marcus know you are getting married?"

"Yes," she replied.

"What did he say?"

"He asked me if I was sure that's what I wanted?"

I waited a moment, took a deep breath.

"And, is this what you want?

"Um, yes," she muttered.

That was a less than resounding response and the fact that she was texting all weekend made me believe she was having conversations with Marcus the whole time she was at my house. I felt like he was trying to prevent the marriage and she was buying into whatever he was saying. Again, I had no proof, only a feeling and intuition.

Later, we prepared a dinner of shrimp kabobs, rice, salad and chicken. She was going to make the rice, but when I saw the way she was going to make it, I just had to open my big mouth.

"Honey, are you boiling the 30 cups of water for an army or for just the six of us," I said, jokingly.

"What do you mean by that?"

That's when the chef in me came out.

"Rice is made with two cups water for every cup of rice."

"I make it my way and I've always done it this way."

"Okay," I acquiesced.

She later went into one of the bedrooms to watch "America's Next Top Model" with her daughters. When her water for the rice started to boil, it was splashing everywhere. I called her, but either she never heard me or she was ignoring me. I looked at the boiling pot and took matters into my own hands.

I measured out the right amount of water to rice and made it the correct way. When the program was over, she came into the kitchen to check the water. I apologized and told her what happened and that I took care of it. Dark clouds were forming around her like a tornado ready to touch down and I could feel it. She said nothing.

Later she joined me on the couch to watch the game. The shear physical attraction to her was unbearable. I leaned over and kissed her face. I caressed her lovely soft brown skin and played with her course, black hair that smelled so fresh and lovely. As I stared at her, I saw a sad, lost look in her eyes. She turned to me and asked, "Why don't you treat me this way all the time?"

The halftime dinner was tense, as she and her kids were completely silent. My brother, Dino, and I, being goof balls, tried to lighten the mood by being silly with little success. It was like a morgue, my brother later would say. There was absolutely no conversation between anyone but my brother and me.

Once the dinner was done, I felt drained, but I refused to buy into the drama of it. The truth was, the kids fed off their mom, so if she was quiet, which she was most of the time, so were they. If mom was talkative and excited about something, they at least smiled and tried to be open to conversation.

This power of influence by Luna was also present when Luna was growing up. She once told me that if she was at the dinner table around friends of her mother and she made a comment or spoke up, her mother would dig her fingernails into Luna's arms to the point that they would bleed. This was her mother's way of saying, "Children should be seen and not heard." She had no idea that she was applying the same law to her kids, although not physically, from what I could so far gather.

Near the end of the game, Luna got up and started cleaning the kitchen.

"Babe, come back, the game's not over yet," I said to her.

She turned a deaf ear.

"Luna, we will take care of the mess later."

She turned to me and said, "I'm not good enough to cook in your kitchen, but I'm good enough to clean it."

She said it loud enough to where my brother Dino heard it and he is hard of hearing. He looked at me with a look of "WTF?" I walked into the kitchen to talk to her and she moved quickly away from me.

"Luna, what's the matter?" I asked.

"I'm not good enough to cook in your kitchen, but I'm good enough to be your maid."

"Luna, stop it. We cook together all the time and you made breakfast this morning," I reminded her.

"Breakfast is nothing. Anyone can do that."

I knew she was in no mood to talk or reason with, so I went back to watch the game. Moments later, I heard her call the kids. When I looked around, they were all headed out the door. No goodbyes, hugs or anything. I got up off the sofa and headed after them. Luna was getting into the driver side of the van.

"What is going on here?"

"Nothing, Stephen, now let me go!" she said emphatically, as she slammed the door in my face.

She only had three drinks all day, so I knew her anger and actions were not alcohol-related and I was not worried about her driving. She started the van and began to pull out of the driveway. I waved goodbye to the kids went back inside. I sat down on the sofa when Dino asked me what happened. Then, before I could answer, all hell broke loose. Luna showed back up and stormed in the house.

"You are driving us home."

"What?" I asked, surprised.

"Stephen, I can't get caught with alcohol on my breath; they will take me to jail if they pull me over."

I understood, but in no way from three in the afternoon until now at eight o'clock would she be drunk on three glasses of wine. In the meantime, because I knew I would be staying in the house, I had much more to drink.

With driving as such a huge part of my job, I could be terminated if I received a ticket or a DUI and I tried to explain this to her. I suggested that she go home in the morning, as that made more sense than either of us going tonight.

"No, I want to go home now and you are driving us," she strongly demanded.

Now, I felt she was using the situation as a power play to make me do as she wished. Luna was a control freak when it came to her kids and her world. She did a damn good job trying to control me and other men through her looks and sexual prowess, but she also was the queen of using guilt to get what she wanted. I decided not to heed her demand. Furthermore, she's acted like an ass the whole weekend, so why should I do anything for her? Then she screamed at me, "You are driving us home!"

By now, I was up to my neck in frustration. I had tried to be the good yogi, I had held back my pent up frustration, but now, I was ready to snap. I had tried hard to make her happy, to the point of draining my own spirit. I knew that dark, miserable experience would be waiting for me in the van, if I drove them home. It had happened many times, especially that fateful time at Enrique's on Memorial Day. Now, being faced with that again, I couldn't bear it.

"I'm not driving you home and I'm not going to be in a place where your kids don't have half a brain to talk to me," I announced.

The minute I spoke those infamous words, I knew I was in trouble. I meant to say, "I don't want to be in a van with people who are upset and angry with nothing to say."

She jumped on my miscue like a rattlesnake.

"What did you just say? Did you say my kids don't have a brain?"

"No, that's not what I meant," I tried to explain.

"Well, I will tell you this: they are smarter than anyone in your family."

"Luna, I didn't mean to say what I did. I know they are intelligent. I'm just frustrated."

There was a moment of silence and it was deafening.

"I can't believe you said that about my kids, you fucker!"

"Luna, I try so hard to talk to you and your kids and I feel like I don't exist. I try to make you guys happy and all you do is look at me like I am an idiot."

"Maybe you are. Do you hear some of the stupid stuff you say?" she interjected.

"Like what? 'Hey girls, how is school? Are you getting good grades? Are there any cute boys?' I try so hard to connect with them and they won't even respond to me, but that is not their fault, it is yours. You have trained them to be robots; they only talk and respond if they get the okay from the all-powerful Oz!"

That was how I saw it. If I asked them a question, they would glance at their mother for permission to speak. At that statement, she approached me in anger. Not knowing where this would go if she got physical, I grabbed the keys out of her hand and said, "Come on, let's go."

I wanted her out of my house. On the way to her apartment, it was like I expected: a morgue. Then, she said something that I still despise her for.

"Kids, Stephen says you guys are stupid and have nothing to say."

Jesus, why did she do that? Now, what will they think of me? I asked myself.

Then, one by one, she called each of their names and had them tell me what they did at school last week. Once all three reported in, she turned arrogantly to me and said, "See Stephen, they can talk."

We got to her place and the kids went inside. I tried letting her know how I felt that I wasn't part of their lives and I wanted to be. She left the van angry and not the least bit sympathetic to me or the relationship I wanted and needed to create with her and her children.

On Wednesday the following week, I had been working in the winery after my normal job at Super Foods. When I got home, I was really beat. She called to tell me she was still angry with me and that she felt things were not working. I told her I felt the same way, but she had to pull the trigger. I was holding true to myself and my promise.

We met a couple a nights later to talk. I went to pick her up and when I got to her door, she cracked it open, and I started to walk in. She closed the door and told me to go wait in the car.

"Sorry?" I asked.

"Go wait in the car," she demanded.

Now I knew how her son must feel: a scolded little boy being told to go to his room. I also wondered if someone else was there, maybe Marcus. Would she have him in her place, with her kids there, while still being involved with me? Crazy thoughts raced through my head. She took forever to get ready and when she came down, I asked her where she wanted to go. She suggested a place that was close to her house and where she sometimes hung out. She knew the owner and bartender.

We had a seat at the bar and almost immediately, she let me know what a horrible person I was. She told me how I never took her shopping, how I never offered to do things for her or bought her things. She told me how I never bought her and her kids groceries. I stopped her there.

"Was I supposed to buy you groceries?"

"I always took stuff up to your house," she stated, boldly.

"Yes, you did because you know I'm a single guy and I don't have a lot of food on hand, let alone stuff that kids like. Also, we both go shopping at the produce market to get stuff for the weekend. What about all the food I bought from my company and gave to you?

She turned away like she didn't want to listen to me.

"The chicken, steaks, tuna, shrimp, cookies, muffins, hamburgers, and everything else I gave you?"

I was always asking her if she needed or wanted anything. As my eyes started to well with tears and frustration, she poked them out.

"You never did anything for us."

I had enough of her lying and so, I stood up for myself.

"What about the times I brought you and the kids medicine and homemade soup when you were sick? The numerous times I made you a bath at my house, complete with a glass of wine, candle light and music? Driving twenty-five minutes each way to pick up and drop off you and the kids because you couldn't drive? Giving you the TV from my bedroom because yours broke? What about taking all of us to the Cowboy Poetry Festival, teaching your kids to shoot a bb gun, going hiking, buying them presents, cooking individual meals for each of them and treating them like my own family? What about helping you find your attorney and getting the van fixed, putting it in my name and getting you insurance? Was all of that nothing?"

"Big deal."

Then, she put another nail in the coffin.

"I paid for all the repairs on the van because I didn't want to owe you anything and yes, you got me the attorney's number, but you never helped me pay for any of his fees or tickets."

Wow, I thought to myself. In one sentence, she said she didn't want to be beholden to me and then, wanted me to pay for her attorney and tickets.

"I'm supposed to pay for your past mistakes of being irresponsible and neglectful?"

At that, she got up, grabbed her purse and left the bar. She always ran away when she didn't have a comeback or want to face the truth. I asked the bartender where she went and he said the restroom. I waited for about ten minutes and she never came back. I called her cell and she picked up.

"Where are you?" I asked

"I'm walking home, Stephen."

I paid the bill, got into my car and went to look for her. There she was, on the street corner, down a few blocks near the shop that fixed the van. I pulled into the lot and waited for her. She got in the car without being prompted. Now, I understood her modus operandi.

This was a game to her. She would throw a fit, want me to come after her, we would fight a little more, then we would make up, make love and all was well until the next time. This was who she was; this is what she was used to. Now, I understood her more than ever and I couldn't handle it. Her life and way of living was completely foreign to me. The way she was raised and her troubled upbringing were very clear now in her methodology.

I got why her ex-husband left her and his own three kids for another woman who had three kids that were not even his. Luna pushed him away. No man in his right mind would leave his own kids for someone else's, especially if that woman was as beautiful Luna was, unless she forced him. Now, I better understood the revolving door of men, as everyone and everything in her life was temporary. Her life was a world of superficial personal relationships that were on and off again and based on the only thing she knew and felt comfortable with: her looks, control and sex.

She railed on me for about twenty minutes in the alleyway where we parked. I was getting tired, as there was nothing I could do or say as she continued to point out my every perceived flaw. I'm controlling, I'm insensitive, and I think I'm better than everyone else. Finally, I had enough and started to drive towards her place.

"Stop! I'm not ready to go yet and I'm not done talking," she demanded.

Tired and drained of all energy and spirit, I looked at her.

"But, I am Luna, I am."

She was angry as hell as I drove up and parked in front of her place. There was silence and then, she said, "I don't know why we couldn't make it in this lifetime."

I was surprised by that statement because of my déjà vu at the hospital.

"Do you want the ring back?" she asked.

I glanced at her hand and the ring was not on her finger.

"No, you keep it. Sell it, throw it away, I don't care," I said, exhausted.

She got out of the car, and walked up to her apartment, never looking back.

I sat there for a few moments, feeling relieved that maybe this was really it. No more making up. No more trying to make an unhappy woman and her family happy. I felt a great release as I drove home with a clear conscience. I felt like I tried my best to make it work. I came to the conclusion that this woman was in need of more help than I could give, that maybe it was not just the negative childhood she had experienced, but maybe something chemical. If her biological mystery father was a drug addict, then maybe she was born affected by this. Maybe she was bipolar or suffered from multiple personality disorder and that was the cause of her ups and downs.

I laughed to myself about her statement, "I don't know why we couldn't make it in this life." Maybe it's because you are insane?

It's interesting how some people can handle certain parts of their lives very well, while other parts are train wrecks. Luna was an excellent worker and her customers loved her. Yet, outside of that world, she, in my opinion, was lost. This was especially true when it came to endearing, true relationships with men.

As far as my friends and family, they felt for me, but were elated that the caustic relationship had come to its finality. Although they would have to endure the days, weeks, and even months of my feeling hurt and confused, they, nonetheless, were thrilled that Stephen, the free spirit, was back.

Asa said something when I was in one of my blue periods.

"My friend, you do not know, at this moment, while you are hurting, what a blessing and a gift it was that she left you this time. Your life would have been a living hell. You are too good of a person and spirit to spend your life trying to make someone else happy; it is not your responsibility. It is her job to work on herself and she has a long, long road ahead."

I could end the chapter of Luna here and I wish I could, but I can't yet. For, what happened next is too painful and odd to ignore.

A Sign from Heaven / Salt In the Wound

After the final breakup, I was still in possession of the van. She called on Sunday, one day before Valentine's Day, to say she needed it back. Since my brother was coming to my house, I told her I would bring it later in the day. At this point, the van was registered and insured to me, so I was liable for anything that happened with it. I dropped it off in her parking space, placed the keys in the center console, and my brother and I drove home. I prayed that she wouldn't try to drive it until she recorded everything in her name.

The next day was Valentine's Day. I got up that morning and made a breakfast of steak and eggs. I placed the skillet into the sink and filled it with water so I could clean it later. As I ate, my mind was on Luna. I even had an impulse to call and say happy Valentine's Day, but she was not my Valentine. We were over. Had I really attempted to call her, my brother, who is 6'4", would have taken me out back for an old-fashioned ass whooping.

As I finished eating, I went to the sink to wash the plates. I glanced at the skillet that was filled with water and to my absolute amazement, the oil and water mixture had formed into the perfect shape of a heart. Of all days to see a heart, Valentine's Day. I took pictures and showed it to friends and people who were into the spiritual side of things and they all were amazed. The question was, what did it mean? Was it a sign that she still loved me or that I still loved her? Or, as one spiritualist put it, "It has nothing to do with love between you and Luna. It manifested and appeared to tell you that God loves you and to love thyself." That left me with much to ponder.

The next day was Tuesday. I went by her place to drop off the release of ownership form, so she could have the van put in her name. She promised, since she had the day off, she would walk the three blocks to the DMV to register it. When I dropped off the van the Sunday before, I had failed to write the mileage down on the form I needed to send to the DMV. I asked her to please call or text me the mileage so I could complete the form. I knew she wouldn't and she didn't, so I needed to make another trip to her place to get the information.

On Wednesday, I went by and the van was gone. In its place was an older, white Lexus. I knew she was at work and so I texted her to ask where the van was.

"A friend of mine had to move some things, so I loaned her the van and in exchange, she left one of her cars for me to use."

I told Luna I still needed the odometer reading off the van and she told me she would get it for me. Later that night, she called me.

"Stephen, there was an issue with the van today."

"What happened? Don't tell me you wrecked it."

"No, I didn't wreck the van. My girlfriend, who was borrowing it, got pulled over by the sheriffs."

"What did she do?

"Nothing, she was just driving it and the sheriffs pulled her over, thinking it was me. Isn't that weird?"

"Why would the police be interested in you enough to follow you around?"

"I don't know."

"Were you in the van with her?"

"No," she replied, calmly.

"Where is the van now?"

"She still has it."

There was a long pause and then she spoke again.

"I have a request of you. Is there any way I can pay for a month of insurance on the van?"

"No, once I reported the van sold or gifted, the insurance was automatically removed."

"You can't extend it for me?"

Why the hell would I do anything for you after all this? I thought to myself.

"My insurance company is not going to insure a vehicle that is not owned by me."

"I haven't recorded it in my name yet."

"Luna, you told me Tuesday on your day off, you were going to do it."

"I know, but I was too tired and I didn't, but I promise I will get it done by this Friday."

I told her again that I could not and would not insure the van for her another day, let alone another month. Something about her needy request, the issue with the sheriffs and the whole story of lending the van to a mysterious friend bugged me.

The next day, Thursday, I went by her place and the van was MIA. The white Lexus was still in its spot. I call her once more and asked her where the van was.

"I don't know why I have to explain myself to you. The van is in the shop for some minor repairs, but there is nothing wrong. It left me stranded because the alternator went out. I understand your concern, but the van is fine."

Oh my God, I thought to myself.

Just the night before, she said her friend still had the van and had been pulled over by the sheriffs. That meant the van was running and seemingly in good shape. Now less than 12 hours later, the van left her stranded, and is in the shop with a bad alternator?

I asked her where the van was being repaired and she refused to tell me. I thought the whole story was beyond suspicious. I had to find out what was going on and, since she was not telling the truth, I needed to do my own investigation.

I called a few friends who frequented this little bar that she would sometimes go to. It was a few blocks from her apartment, so if she got tipsy, she could walk home. She also went there with people from work occasionally to see a friend's band.

I asked if they had seen her and, if so, was she hanging with anyone. My intuition told me that Marcus was involved in this somehow, but my heart told me that she wouldn't be with another man only a few days after breaking off our engagement. After all, she said she loved me more than any man in her life. Rationally, she wouldn't drag her kids into another affair that quick after being with me, would she? My sources confirmed my intuition.

"Yes, she has been seen with Marcus a few times in the bar," my friend informed me.

"What kind of car does he drive?" I asked.

"He drives an older, white Lexus."

My heart fell to my stomach. Before I could ask anything else, she continued.

"Stephen, I want to tell you something. This guy is a scum bag. He has a girlfriend, but when she is away, he hits on everything in sight. The times they have been in the bar together, they were all over each other and I know who he is and trust me, they have had sex. So, do yourself a favor and get checked. He has screwed so many women, who knows what he might have."

So there it was. His car was parked at her place only a few days after breaking off our engagement. I knew more than ever I was dealing with a lying, irresponsible, childish, ethically-challenged woman.

Like the old slogan for the *National Enquirer* said, "Inquiring minds want to know" and since Luna would never tell me the real story, I had to play detective. I called people I knew in the law enforcement side of Santa Clarita. Though they could not divulge everything, they told me that her nearly getting arrested by the CHP and the $1,200 she had to pay for a ticket smelled of a DUI, one that may have truly have been part of the "on the cell phone" ticket she may have lied to me about.

Recently, I found out that only days after returning the van to her, she was driving it and got pulled over. The sheriffs gave her a ticket for the infraction and a citation for not having insurance. Now, I more clearly understood why she wanted me to extend the insurance coverage. So there was no mystery woman borrowing the van.

To repeat what I had written before near the start of this book, the truth can hurt, but a lie can be so much more damaging, for after a lie is uncovered, one must question what else the person may have lied about. Luna was a habitual liar and now, it was in my face.

After our final demise, common friends told me about how, when she would tell a story they knew was a lie, they would challenge her on it. Now, they said the stories and lies were so prevalent that they would just laugh and shake their heads. Luna also took my kids off her friends list on Facebook, an act that hurt my son's feelings quite a bit, especially after she said that she loved my kids as her own. But, once she was done with me, she threw the kids away, as well.

The grape that most fit Luna? A Port style, late harvest Zinfandel or Syrah. A wine made from either overripe fruit or sometimes fortified with alcohol. It is a viscous, high-octane, sexy, alluring wine, with deep, dark berry flavors and residual sweetness and alcohol that packs a punch. Need I say more?

In Retrospect

In closing the chapter about Luna (and this chapter of my life), I now know, as I am a spiritual being, that we attract things based on our vibrations. Put into relationship terms, we pull all the things we truly want towards us like a large magnet if we are sure and focused in our desires. But, we also attract those things we do not want, if we are unsure or unclear.

The Universe does not hear negatives, only the authentic true request. So, this leads me to think that we need to not only be very careful what we wish for or put energy into, but also how we do it.

One last point: we can also be given a person, a problem or a gift in order to experience it, to help our soul grow and make different or better choices in the future. I truly feel Luna came into my life for me to experience her and her life. I can't truly blame her for all her craziness, as she was simply a product of her difficult childhood and self-made choices.

Yet, I also know I never want to go through anything like this again. I feel I have learned my lesson and that no one can really help anyone else unless that person wants to change so badly that they take action to do so. I love the song by Rachael Yamagata, "You Won't Let Me", which talks about the very same, sad thing.

Sometimes, a person has to reach rock bottom in order to see the way up, as well as the hard and painful work that must be done to get off the hamster wheel. Not many people choose that option and yet, I believe we can choose to change our lives whenever we wish to.

Luna was the most beautiful, sexually intriguing and yet, psychologically-challenged woman I have ever met in my life. Yet still, I felt compelled to love her and her kids and I gave it my all. Though flawed at times, I worked at us because I was taught to never give up and to never quit people or things that you are committed to. Even the times that I broke it off with her were to make her see that she could not continue to act like she was and still forge a solid, beautiful relationship with me. I felt that if she cared enough for me and for us, she would make those corrections to herself, in order to make things work. She couldn't.

Giving up means failure to me. Was that attitude bequeathed to me from my parents or something I was born with? I don't know. But, I hated losing. Even if what I lost was not all that important, my true nature was to win and to be good at every damn thing I did. Although I had mellowed a lot in my older years, that remnant of Stephen was still present during my time with Luna.

I do know that my parents tried for a long time to have a child and had considered adopting before I finally arrived. They, I felt, expected a great deal out of me, especially being the first born. They told me many times that kids my age and younger looked up to me as a role model and a leader. My mother used to call me "Super Stud" because I was capable of anything I set my mind to. Maybe that's one of the reasons I tried so hard to make this difficult relationship work, even when all the chips were down. I didn't want to fail.

Friends, family, and my ex-wife can tell you that I have always been stubborn and hard-headed when it came to getting what I wanted and, by God, most of the time, I got it, even though it was not always good for me. I wanted Luna to be what I thought her capable of. Yet, she was always going to be exactly what and who she was. So this masquerade was not just about her changing her life by being with me; it was a lesson about me letting go of any demands or impossible expectations.

Winning her unconditional love was a challenge for me, as I had heard she had dated and bedded a lot of men and I was determined to be the last one. I think everyone would like to think they are "it" and "the one." I wanted to be everything in her eyes and, for a short time, I thought I was. But I wasn't.

Why was I so intent on making this work when my own brother, Dino, said it was like putting a square peg in a round hole? Because, damn it, I am Stephen Hemmert and I can do anything. Well, no I can't and sadly, I couldn't. This was a lesson that taught me that sometimes, I do fail and that this is real life and it can be humbling. In fact, we all fail, at some point, and I am no better or any different than anyone else, regardless of what my ego and confidence may say. But, I also want to add that underneath all the anger, hurt and rubble. I saw that Luna was a beautiful soul. Don't ask me how. I don't know, I just sensed it or maybe, I wanted to believe so.

In my heart, I believe that there are people in life who we are destined to love and yet, this does not translate to being with them. In this vast world of souls, it is quite understandable that we will meet, and maybe love, many of them. Some will rock our worlds and some will provide us peace and tranquility. Some will hold us where we are and some will cause us to grow. If our existence here on Earth is to gain knowledge and experience to once again become one with God, then constant contrast of desires and growth must take place. Luna was the catalyst for more spiritual and mental growth than any woman in my life. For that, I thank her.

Looking back, I sadly realize that I meant absolutely nothing to her. I was just another guy and her actions at the end of our engagement proved that. She never truly loved me, as she had no idea of what love is for she does not love herself. When I unconditionally opened my heart and home to her, she couldn't and wouldn't accept it. It was too close to becoming a reality that someone could love and accept her and her children as they were. She was used to drama, chaos and chasing men and relationships that would always be doomed to fail.

I now painfully understand what I never did before: the addict/victim relationship. Luna was like a drug to me, an addiction that, many months later, still lingered inside my soul. And it is true, the sexual intimacy I experienced with her is the hardest to flush from my conscience.

I understand, through the grapevine, that Marcus broke it off with her only a few weeks after she got back with him and that she's already been with another guy very shortly after that, followed by another, then another. I thought about her children, being dragged along for the ride through each relationship. I know this is not my battle, my war, nor my life, and that there is nothing I can or should do about it. But, when I meditate every night and morning, she and her kids are there. I place a white light around them and ask God to watch over them.

For my own sanity, I have destroyed and thrown away all pictures of her, but even with all of that, I can't let go of her beautiful face or the remembrance of the delicate kisses she placed upon my lips. In retrospect, should I? Are these not reminders of what we should expect to receive from someone we are in love with?

Having to see her at work is difficult because every time I do, I wish to God that things could have been different. Spiritually, I know God and the Universe have lined up a new soul for me to experience and love. And yet, in my moments of human weakness, I question why I was destined to meet a soul whose face seems so ancient and whose physical vibrations so closely matched mine and yet, we cannot be together.

The Lesson: Let Intuition Be Your Guide

G od gave us a brain to use in conjunction with our instinct and our heart. I believe that the brain can truly talk us into and out of anything and that our ancient use of intuition has taken a backseat to the power of the mind and the ego. If you remember, I mentioned what I felt intuitively about Luna in the very beginning when I met her and yet, my mind, ego and physical arousal of her overruled my gut instinct. I know now, more than ever, to give more credence to my God-given intuitive nature.

In the meantime, my mind is still constantly chatting away at me. It blamed much of the collapse of the relationship with Luna on me because I couldn't make her happy or do enough. In retrospect, I do bear some responsibility, as the failure in a relationship is never completely one-sided. But, why should I beat myself up about this? Why do most of us hear the chatter and negative thoughts inside our head long after a breakup? Why do we cling to the past when the present moment and the possible future await us?

It's because we fall into a position of wanting what is or was comfortable. The future is scary and therefore, unpredictable. So, we cling to what we know, whether it is good or bad. Esther and Jerry Hicks explain this very well in their book, *The Astonishing Power of Emotions.*

They say in Example 29, "My lover left me." "Most people who want a relationship believe that a mediocre relationship is better than none at all. But, we do not agree with that. In other words, since the potential for a glorious relationship always exists, we never encourage settling for less." We also have to be in alignment with ourselves and believe that we are worthy of a better, more fulfilling and rewarding relationship.

For all my spiritual understanding and knowledge, I failed to recognize the inevitable signs of my own ego. How on Earth can anyone save or fix anyone else? You can't; they have to be willing to do the work themselves and bring themselves into alignment. Although both Luna and I wanted this relationship to be, it simply could not be. We were both passionate, sexual and giving people, but we were simply in different emotional, psychological and spiritual places.

I knew I had to forgive her and the things she did that hurt me, but, more importantly, I had to forgive myself. No one can make you feel anything but what you allow yourself to feel and I allowed her to cause me hurt, pain, and anguish. I had to forgive myself for going there.

Over time through friends, meditation and self-introspection, I was able to shake off the shackles of shame and responsibility and begin to clear my spirit of her. One way of clarity was to seek advice from a talented Tarot reader I know who nailed our situation to a T. He stated that my birth date and sign shows humor, light, love and caring for people. Luna's sign showed darkness, lies, hurt and pain.

"My friend, stay far away from her, she is like a psychic vampire. She will drain your spirit and soul of everything you possess."

These words hit home, as they had already occurred.

"Let her go," he said. "She will never change and will continue on the path she is on, with or without you."

And So It Goes

If you are drained after reading the Luna segment of the book, I did my job, as this relationship drained the life out of me. I felt so drained, in fact, that I have lost all my sexual desires and have temporally closed off my heart. I feel like I wasted the passion of my soul on a woman who only saw or comprehended lust as love. Of course, nothing is ever really wasted, but I think we all get to a point where we are tired and where we need to retreat, recharge, and reflect, and that is where I am.

My mother used to warn me about trying to make things work that just weren't meant to be. She would look at me and, with her Southern drawl say, "Stephen, you try so hard to push the river, when it flows perfectly by itself."

She was absolutely right. And so, I need to further investigate why I do what I do. Why not let my heart or intuition be my guide? To accept what is or isn't and try not to make it something it can't be.

Could it be that the whole purpose of what I have experienced and gone through over the past few years of dating, is to simply recognize my choices in women and to see the contrasts which will further hone my future choices? To choose a woman that will be much closer to my truest and deepest desires? Also, these past few years taught me to appreciate them for who they are and who they are not. I couldn't have written this book without these interesting and sometimes strange women and spirits.

Maybe this life is not about falling in love with everything that's right or perfect in a person, but to gain greater compassion and love in experiencing that which isn't. Maybe, it's about the deeper discovery of self. To know and to love yourself, other than God, is the greatest thing one can do and must happen before you find your perfect match or soul mate.

Every woman I was able to share time with taught me something. Not just about them or about life, but about myself. In this phase of my life I learned confidence and how to flirt and attract women. I was excited emotionally and physically by some and completely turned off by others. I also learned to laugh at my mistakes and the craziness that surrounded me. There were times I felt like I was in an episode of Seinfeld where everyone, including myself was somehow hilariously dysfunctional. In retrospect, I would not trade those experiences for anything in the world.

So spiritually, emotionally and mentally, I went on a journey, an exploration of life and love, which, as of the closing of this book, still continues. Yes, I still am attracted to women and they still seemed to be attracted to me. But, now what? What has God and the Universe planned for me?

I would like to close this book with a positive statement of hope from *The Astonishing Power of Emotions* by Jerry and Esther Hicks. "Many people work very hard to try and make things work out. But we want you to understand that when you work to bring yourself into alignment with YOU rather than into alignment with what someone else wants you to be, then the universe will bring you the match. Just work to maintain your alignment and the Universe will deliver to you partners who are aligned. It is Law."

Addendum

Since finishing this book in March of 2012, Mye and I have once again begun talking to each other. Interestingly enough, we have found that even three years later, we still share a strong connection and feeling for each other. I plan to travel to Jamaica soon and I can only hope we can pickup where we left off. I know they say you can never go back, but was this really every finished between us? I promise to go there with an open mind and heart. Will something come of this? Only heaven knows.

Made in the USA
San Bernardino, CA
24 February 2019